B890

GEOGRAPHY

Prepared for the course team by Peter Dicken
with contributions by Allan Plath

MBA

International Enterprise

The Open
University

BUSINESS
SCHOOL

OPEN UNIVERSITY COURSE TEAM

Core group

Dr Allan Plath, *Course Team Chair*

Mr Jon Billsberry, *Critical Reader*

Mr Martin Brazier, *Graphic Designer*

Mr Eric Cassells, *Author*

Dr Timothy Clark, *Author*

Ms Karen Dolan, *Course Manager*

Mrs Shirley Eley, *Course Team Assistant*

Ms Ann Falkner, *Liaison Librarian*

Ms Julie Fletcher, *Editor*

Mr Mike Green, *Critical Reader*

Mrs Cherry Harris, *Course Team Assistant*

Dr Nick Heap, *Author*

Mr Roy Lawrance, *Graphic Artist*

Dr Richard Mole, *Production Director, OUBS*

Prof. Derek Pugh, *Author*

Prof. Janette Rutterford, *Author*

Ms Linda Smith, *Project Controller*

Prof. Andrew Thomson, *Author*

Mr Steve Wilkinson, *BBC Series Producer*

External consultants

Dr Jim Attridge, *Critical Reader*

Dr David Barnes, *Author*

Prof. Peter Dicken, *Author*

Prof. John Drew, *Author and Editor of the Reader*

Prof. Nigel Grimwade, *Author*

Prof. Malcolm Hill, *Author*

Prof. Paul Iles, *Author*

Mr Ian McCall, *Author*

Dr David Silk, *Author*

Dr Steve Tallman, *Author*

Prof. Monir Tayeb, *Author*

Developmental testers

Ms Barbara Awuku-Asabre

Mr Ian Cooley

Dr Alan Eggleston

Mr David Milton

Mr Roy Needham

Mr Fred Thomson

External assessors

Prof. Dr Pervez N. Ghauri, *University of Groningen, The Netherlands*

Prof. Simon Coke, *Edinburgh University Management School, Edinburgh*

The Open University, Walton Hall, Milton Keynes MK7 6AA

First published 1995, second edition 1999, reprinted 2001

Edited, designed and typeset by The Open University.

Printed in the United Kingdom by Selwood Printing Ltd, Burgess Hill, West Sussex.

ISBN 0 7492 7678 9

For further information on Open University Business School courses and the Certificate, Diploma and MBA programmes, please contact the Course Sales Development Centre, The Open University, PO Box 222, Walton Hall, Milton Keynes MK7 6YY (tel: 01908 653449).

oubs.open.ac.uk

2.3

19044B/b890gui2.3

CONTENTS

INTRODUCTION

BACKGROUND TO THE UNIT

This is the last unit of the first part of the course (Diversity). The unit should be thought of as the 'capstone' of the first part of the course, because it integrates a large number of ideas from previous units.

But the unit is more than just a summary, reiteration or synthesis of previous concepts. Geography adds its own perspective to the topic of Diversity and, in doing so, provides us with a different view of the patterns of international enterprise.

Many of you will have studied geography at school. Your recollections of what geography means will probably be of the kind catered for in the game Trivial Pursuit: 'What is the capital of country X?' 'What is the largest country in continent Y?' 'Which is colder, the North Pole or the South Pole?' Being able to answer these questions may give you some glory and satisfaction at a party but how does it help you, as a businessperson, to understand the highly competitive world in which you have to make your living? In that sense, does geography matter?

The basic message of this unit is that geography matters a great deal. Indeed, the message is stronger than that. International business is intrinsically geographical – even though most of the standard textbooks in international business appear to ignore it. I say 'appear' because a great deal of the material of these texts is, in fact, geographical. Unfortunately, most of the texts that do deal explicitly with the geographical dimension adopt a very traditional perspective. For example, Daniels and Radebaugh write as follows:

> A grasp of *geography* is important because it helps managers to determine the location, quantity, and quality of the world's resources and their availability for exploitation. The distribution of these resources gives rise to the production of different products and services in different parts of the world ... Geographical barriers such as high mountains, vast deserts, and inhospitable jungles affect communication and distribution channels for companies in much of the world's economy. Human population distribution around the world and the impact of human activity on the environment exert a strong influence on international business relationships.
>
> *(Daniels and Radebaugh, 1989, p. 11)*

The emphasis here is essentially descriptive. Indeed, it isn't very different from the Trivial Pursuit kind of geography. All you need is a good atlas and a reference book telling you where things – especially physical things – are located. This is fine as far as it goes because such geographical knowledge is important – but it really does not go far enough. If that is all that geography means then it would be very hard to justify its inclusion as a substantive unit in this course.

A rather more sophisticated geographical perspective is adopted by Robock and Simmonds in their standard text *International Business and Multinational Enterprises*. They develop what they call a geobusiness model which:

> ... incorporates a large number of key variables whose *interaction* changes the geographical source and destination of inter-nation business

activity. It recognizes that the individual enterprise is the motive force and that international business patterns are shaped by the adjustments of specific enterprises, operating competitively over a range of natural environments to survive and grow. The variables of the model can be grouped under three headings: (1) conditioning variables; (2) motivational variables; and (3) control variables ...

(Robock and Simmonds, 1989, p. 51)

Table 1	The geobusiness model
Conditioning variables	
Product-specific	Product and factor requirements, technology and production characteristics
Country-specific	(a) National market demands
	(b) Disparities in natural and human resource endowments
	(c) Disparities in technological, cultural, institutional, economic and political environments
Inter-nation	International financial, trade, transportation, and communication systems, and agreements that affect the spatial movement of information, money, goods, people, etc.
Motivational variables	
Firm-specific	Geographical perception and resource availability
Competitive	The relative competitive position of individual enterprises and competitor moves and threats
Strategy	Internalization advantages and disadvantages
Control variables	
Country-specific	Administrative actions, laws and policies of home country and host country governments that directly or indirectly influence international business through positive incentives and/or negative controls
Inter-nation	International agreements, treaties and codes of conduct directly affecting the pattern of international business

(Source: Robock and Simmonds, 1989, p. 51)

Table 1 provides the details of this geobusiness model. The kinds of geographical variables included are very different from those implied in the earlier, more traditional, perspective reflected in the quotation from Daniels and Radebaugh. Robock and Simmonds's model takes us much closer to an understanding of the importance of a geographical perspective in international business.

However, most of their variables are dealt with separately in other units of this course. So, you may ask, why repeat them here? The basic answer is: one of the most important components of a geographical perspective is that it emphasizes the *interaction* between economic, social, political and cultural factors in specific places. It is the *particular assemblage* which distinguishes one place, area or region from another and which provides the 'soil' within which businesses are embedded. *Place*, therefore, is a fundamental geographical variable which has profound implications for businesses of all kinds. A second, related, fundamental geographical variable is *location*. The location decision is explicitly geographical but it is important to realize that it is not so much *absolute* location that matters (that is, the precise physical co-ordinates on the map) as *relative* location. In that respect, *distance* between locations and between places is clearly fundamental although again it is relative, not absolute, distance that matters.

The important point about a geographical perspective, then, is not that it is concerned with where things like natural resources, cities, populations and so on are in any absolute sense. It is the fact that it is concerned with their spatial relationships and connectedness (expressed in terms of relative distances) and their distinctive assemblage in specific places. Geography, therefore, is primarily about space and about place, and about the processes involved. All the processes with which social scientists and businesses are concerned are intrinsically geographical; they all occur in geographical space and place, and are therefore influenced by this fact. At the same time, they all contribute towards changing the geography of the world in which they operate. It is important to emphasize this point because, too often, economists, political scientists and, to a lesser extent, sociologists pursue their work as if the phenomena they are studying exist on the head of a pin or as if we all live in some kind of spaceless wonderland. But, as Porter, one of the leading writers on contemporary business, has observed, 'While economic geography has not been seen as a core discipline in economics, my research suggests that it should be' (Porter, 1990, p. 791).

Space and place are themselves rather abstract concepts; they must be made concrete by the specification of geographical scale. Scale itself, of course, is a continuum, ranging from the global at one extreme to the local at the other. It is these two scales that are currently the focus of much debate in the international business strategy literature: should firms 'go global' or should they 'go local' or should they try to combine the two and 'glocalize'? But when we look more closely at the global–local question we find that it is more complex than it appears at first sight; both terms are often used very loosely and inconsistently.

'Going global' or 'globalizing' means a great deal more than merely the geographical dispersal of operations across a number of national boundaries. Geographical dispersion is the process of internationalization, whereas globalization is qualitatively different: it is a more advanced and more complex process which involves functional integration between internationally dispersed operations. At the other end of the geographical scale, the term 'local' or 'localizing' is also subject to differing interpretations. To the international business enterprise or the transnational corporation (TNC), 'local' tends to be equated with particular countries: 'local' equals 'national'. But to the kind of local community in which each of us lives, 'local' signifies a much smaller geographical scale. It is this 'seriously local' scale which concerns primarily the individual, the family, the household, the local politician and the local economic development officer. But, of course, the 'seriously local' is embedded within the national political, economic, social and cultural system. Thus, in trying to understand the relationships between geography and international business we need to be sensitive to at least three geographical scales – the global, the national and the local – and to the interactions between them. Their basic characteristics are shown in Figure 1 (overleaf).

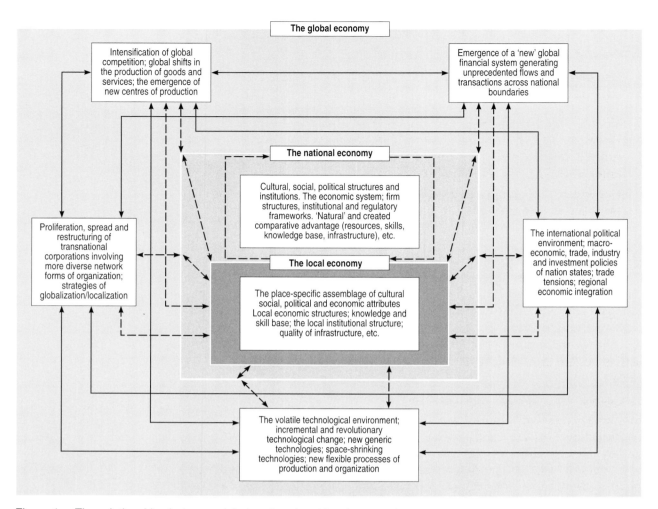

Figure 1   The relationships between global, national and local economies

Despite the rather lurid statements of writers such as Kenichi Ohmae or Robert Reich, international business is not 'placeless'. All business firms are 'produced' in specific places and are, therefore, embedded in particular economic, political, social, cultural and cognitive milieux. When such firms engage in operations outside their home countries they carry with them some of the attributes of their home environment. As they locate in other countries they become locally embedded there to varying degrees and take on some of the characteristics of the host environment. This interplay between international firms and places is a key element in understanding international business.

AIMS AND OBJECTIVES

The aim of this unit is to:

- Demonstrate the fundamental role played by geography in international enterprise.

When you have completed this unit, you should be able to:

- Understand how the basic geographical variables of location, distance, space and place affect the ways in which international business enterprises are organized and operate.
- Understand the geographical distribution and dynamics of human population and their implications for product and labour markets.

OVERVIEW OF THE UNIT

This unit is organized into three sections. In Section 1, you will see how foreign direct investment (FDI) has changed over time. In this section, I will argue that most FDI takes place between industrialized countries, and that the 'home' countries of firms exert considerable influence on their activities. The argument here will concern the aggregate behaviour of firms.

In Section 2, I will look at the ways in which firms geographically organize themselves and the ways in which geography influences the relationships between firms. In this section, the production (or value-added) chain will be used to focus attention on three aspects of a firm. These are the firm's technology, its strategic orientation, and the political environments in which it operates. I will argue that each element in the production chain has specific locational requirements that may result in either geographically concentrated or geographically dispersed patterns of location. In this section, I will also show how geography shapes and changes the relationships between organizations, for example, suppliers and customers.

In Section 3, I will explore the geography of population and human resources, and the implications of this for product and labour markets.

1 THE GEOGRAPHY OF INTERNATIONAL ENTERPRISE

1.1 THE GROWTH OF FOREIGN DIRECT INVESTMENT

One of the most useful indicators of the geography of international business is the data collected by virtually all national governments on the flows and stocks of FDI. Although there are considerable variations in the quality and coverage of such data they provide the best available general picture of the growth and geographical diversification of international business activity.

A major change has been occurring in the forces generating international integration in the world economy. For most of the post-war period, it was the growth of *world trade* which was the major force linking national economies (and, of course, local economies as well). It now appears that it is the *investment decisions of international enterprises*, as reflected in the FDI data, which have become the major force connecting different parts of the world. In fact, because international enterprises are themselves responsible for a very large proportion of world trade (much of this as intra-firm transactions) their global significance has become even more marked.

1.2 GEOGRAPHICAL ORIGINS AND DESTINATIONS OF FOREIGN DIRECT INVESTMENT

Geographical origins of FDI: the old and the new

Foreign direct investment originates overwhelmingly from the developed market economies and is heavily concentrated within the global triad of North America, Europe and Japan (Figure 2).

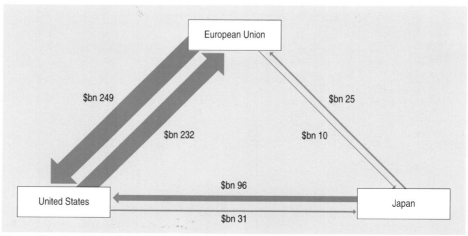

Figure 2   Concentration of foreign direct investment in global triad (Dicken, 1998, p. 61)

But within the triad there are some very important differences. Figure 2 illustrates FDI trends among the leading developed country sources. For most of its history, world foreign direct investment has been overwhelmingly dominated by TNCs from the United States, the United Kingdom and one or two continental European countries. From the 1950s to the mid-1970s, US firms accounted for between 40 and 50 per cent of the world total. In 1960, US and UK TNCs made up two-thirds of the world total. But although TNCs from both countries have continued to invest heavily overseas, other countries' outward investment has increased more rapidly. By 1985, the combined US–UK share of the world total had fallen to around half. Conversely, the German share of the total increased from 1.2 to 8.8 per cent, while Japan's share had grown even more sharply, from 0.7 to 6.5 per cent. From being a very minor player in terms of foreign direct investment in 1960, and not especially important in 1975, Japan had surged up the league table to fourth place by 1985.

1985 marked a major acceleration in the growth of world FDI to unprecedented levels. In that acceleration, Japan was undoubtedly the leading player. Japanese outward direct investment grew from $44 billion in 1985 to $306 billion by 1995 (even though there was a pronounced slackening in the rate of growth in the early 1990s). Comparison with the UK underlines the dramatic change in Japan's global position since 1960. In that year, Japan's share of the world FDI total – 0.7 per cent – was a miniscule one-twenty-sixth of that of the UK (18.3 per cent). In 1995, Japan accounted for 11.2 per cent of the world FDI total, virtually the same as the United Kingdom. In contrast to Japan, Germany's share of the world FDI total has remained virtually unchanged since 1985 at just under 9 per cent, although in 1997/98 there was a dramatic upsurge in German overseas investment, especially through merger and acquisition (examples include the Mercedes Benz merger with Chrysler, Bertelsmann's takeover of Random House, Siemens acquisition of Westinghouse and the battle for Rolls Royce between Volkswagen and BMW).

Of course, it must be emphasized that these are all shares of a much larger total. Foreign direct investment from virtually all developed economies is now very much larger in absolute terms than ever before. A more recent, and potentially highly significant, development is the emergence of TNCs from developing countries. In 1960, approximately 99 per cent of world FDI came from the developed economies. By 1995 around 8 per cent of world FDI originated from developing countries. As yet, only a small number of developing countries is involved. Four-fifths of all developing country FDI originates from just seven countries. Six of those seven are Asian NICs (newly industrialized countries), as Figure 3 overleaf shows. However, though modest in scale, this is undoubtedly the harbinger of an important new development. Despite recent economic difficulties, the world's population of TNCs is not only growing very rapidly, but also there has been a marked increase in the geographical diversity of its origins in ways which cut across the old international division of labour.

Geographical destinations of FDI: increasing interpenetration

As well as relative shifts in the geographical origins of foreign direct investment, equally significant, but very different, shifts have been occurring in its geographical destinations. The geographical structure of FDI has become far more complex in recent years, a further indication

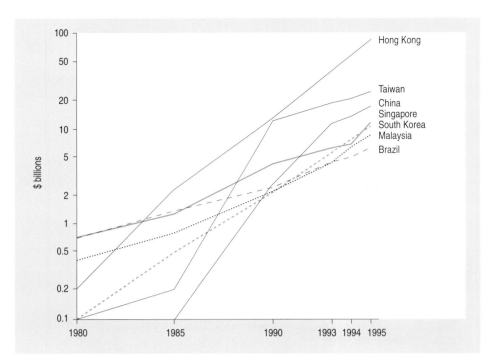

Figure 3   Foreign direct investment from newly industrializing economies, 1980–1995 (Dicken, 1998, p. 45)

of increased interconnectedness within the global economy. Figure 4 maps the overall pattern of the origins and destinations of FDI stocks for 1995. Despite recent developments, the geographical destinations of foreign direct investment are still strongly concentrated in the developed market economies. Indeed, this developed country bias has increased rather than decreased. In 1938, 66 per cent of the world's foreign direct investment went to the developing countries; by 1995 this share had fallen to only 26 per cent. Thus, the developed market economies are not only the dominant source of transnational investment, with 92 per cent of the total, but also the dominant destination. Three-quarters of all FDI in the world in the mid-1990s was located in the developed market economies.

Within that highly concentrated structure the detailed distribution of FDI has changed very considerably. During the 1950s and 1960s it was reasonable to distinguish between those countries that were primarily sources of FDI and those that were primarily destinations for FDI. Among the developed economies – with the notable exception of Japan – that distinction no longer applies. As Figure 4 shows, virtually all developed economies have substantial outward *and* inward direct investment. If we measure this as a simple FDI ratio (outward FDI/inward FDI) then a value of 1.0 would signify an exact balance between outward and inward investment. With just four exceptions, all the countries of Western Europe and North America had FDI ratios within the range 0.8 and 1.5 in 1995. The exceptions were Germany (1.75), Sweden (1.9), Finland (2.2) and Switzerland (2.5). What these patterns imply, in fact, is a high degree of *cross-investment* between the major developed market economies: each is investing in each other's home territory.

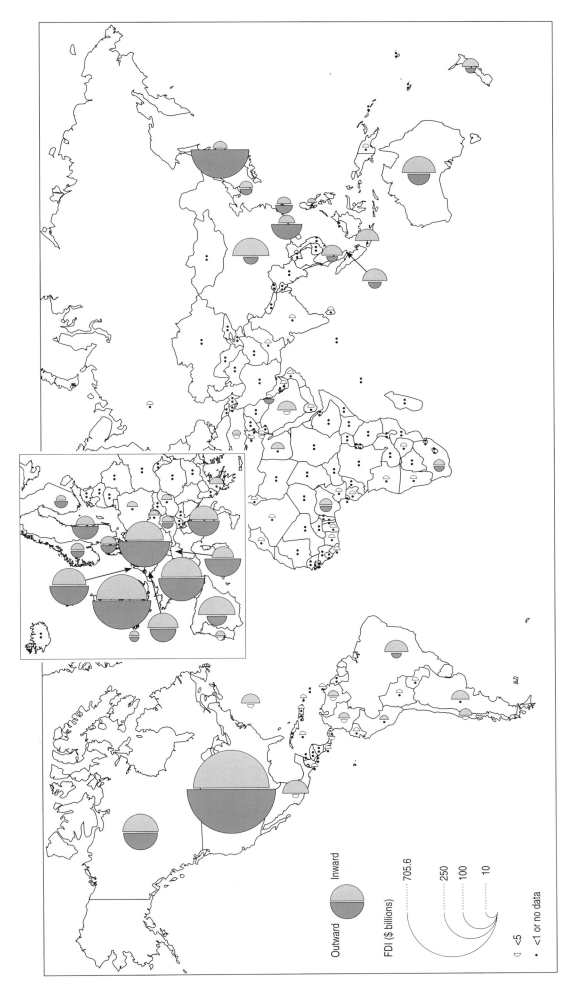

Figure 4   The world map of foreign direct investment, 1995 (Dicken, 1998, p. 46)

Within this general increase in interpenetration of FDI between developed economies, three distinctive features stand out:

- *The dramatic change in the position of the United States as a host country for FDI.* For every leading investing country, the United States became significantly more important as firms from Europe, Japan and, more recently, some East Asian NIEs reoriented the geographical focus of their overseas direct investments.

- *The continuation of Europe's attractiveness to inward investment.* Western Europe's share of total inward investment fell quite substantially between 1975 and 1985 (from 41 per cent of the world total to 33 per cent). But by the mid-1990s, its share had risen again to 41 per cent. The transformation of the political situation in Central and Eastern Europe is also leading to the growth of FDI in these economies although, as yet, the volumes are relatively small. In 1995, only 1.2 per cent of world inward FDI was located in Central and Eastern Europe. However, this represented a ten-fold increase over the position in 1990.

- *The persisting asymmetry of Japan's FDI position.* While the US direct investment position has been transformed from one of being overwhelmingly a home country for FDI to one in which the ratio of outward to inward investment is almost in balance, the same certainly cannot be said of Japan. While Japanese outward investment has grown spectacularly, there has been only very limited growth of inward investment. Along with trade frictions, this huge imbalance in the Japanese direct investment account continues to cause major concern among businesses and policy-makers in the West.

As we have seen, the developing countries as a whole are host to only one-quarter of world FDI. Within that relatively small share there is a very high level of concentration in a small number of countries. Figure 4 shows that inward FDI is minuscule in the majority of developing countries. There is a clear regional dimension to this. Africa's share of the developing countries' total had declined to a mere 8.6 per cent by 1995. Latin America's share had fallen to 33 per cent. In contrast, the Asian share had increased more than two-and-a-half times, from 21 per cent in 1975 to 58 per cent in 1995. A mere ten countries account for more than two-thirds of all FDI in developing countries. Six of these are in Asia, including by far the largest host country – China. Indeed, the extent to which FDI in China has grown since the early 1980s is nothing short of spectacular.

Statistics on the scale of FDI are important in showing us the pronounced geographical variations in destinations. But they tell us nothing about how important such investment is to an individual host economy. In fact, such importance varies enormously from one country to another. One measure of relative domestic importance of inward FDI is to compare it to a country's gross domestic product (GDP). Table 2 shows that for developed countries as a whole, inward FDI constituted around 9 per cent of GDP in 1994. For Western Europe, the share was much higher at 13 per cent. Within Europe, FDI was most significant as a share of GDP in Belgium-Luxembourg (32 per cent), the Netherlands (28 per cent), Spain (25 per cent), Greece (23.5 per cent) and the United Kingdom (20.9 per cent). In North America, there was a pronounced contrast between Canada (where FDI contributed 19 per cent of GDP) and the United States (7.5 per cent). Not surprisingly we find the lowest contribution of all in the case of Japan (0.4 per cent).

Table 2   Inward foreign direct investment as a share of Gross Domestic Product, 1994

	Share of GDP (%)		Share of GDP (%)
Developed countries	8.6	*Developing countries*	12.5
Belgium-Luxembg	31.7	Singapore	72.8
Netherlands	27.7	Malaysia	46.2
Spain	25.0	Indonesia	26.5
Greece	23.5	Hong Kong	20.5
United Kingdom	20.9	Chile	19.2
Canada	19.2	China	17.9
Denmark	12.6	Mexico	14.4
France	10.7	Thailand	10.1
Ireland	10.3	Philippines	8.3
Sweden	9.7	Argentina	8.1
United States	7.5	Brazil	8.0
Germany	6.8	Taiwan	6.6
Portugal	6.6	Pakistan	6.0
Finland	5.9	South Korea	3.3
Italy	5.9	India	0.9
Japan	0.4	Bangladesh	0.7

(Source: Dicken, 1998, p. 48)

Similar variation in the relative significance of foreign penetration is evident among developing countries. In Latin America, foreign firms are especially important to the economies of Mexico (14 per cent of GDP) and Chile (19 per cent). Within Asia the range is especially wide. Foreign firms are dominant in the economy of Singapore (73 per cent of GDP), extremely significant in Malaysia (46 per cent), Indonesia (26.5 per cent) and Hong Kong (20.5 per cent), and significant in China (18 per cent). But in Taiwan, inward FDI contributed only 6.6 per cent of GDP and a mere 3.3 per cent in South Korea.

1.3   HOME COUNTRY INFLUENCE: THE NATIONAL CHARACTERISTICS OF INTERNATIONAL ENTERPRISES

There is a popular view that international enterprises, especially the very large global corporations, are all the same. Even in the academic literature there is a view that the pressures of operating in a globally competitive environment are creating a uniformity of strategy and structure among international firms. It is these kinds of viewpoint that project the notion that international enterprises are 'placeless', have no ties to specific places, and are constantly on the move seeking out new investments and closing down those which are no longer needed.

For example, both Robert Reich and Kenichi Ohmae (whose stage theory of internationalization you saw in the Introduction) adopt the viewpoint that international enterprises have, in effect, become – or are becoming – 'denationalized'. Reich claims in *The Work of Nations* (1991) that, as a result of current transformations, there will be no 'national corporations'. Ohmae, in his book *The Borderless World* (1990), argues that in the global corporation 'country of origin does not matter. Location of headquarters does not matter. The products for which you are responsible and the company you serve have become denationalized' (p. 94). This is very much the Utopian perspective of the international business guru. It is a misleading interpretation of the real world.

A more realistic picture is painted by Hu (1992). He suggests the following criteria for evaluating the nature of international enterprises.

- In which nation or nations is the bulk of the firm's assets and people located?

- By whom are the local subsidiaries owned and controlled, and in which nation is the parent company owned and controlled?

- What is the nationality of the senior positions (executive and board posts) at the parent company, and what is the nationality of the most important decision makers at the subsidiaries in host nations?

- What is the legal nationality of the parent company? To whom would the group as a whole turn for diplomatic protection and political support in case of need?

- Which is the nation where tax authorities can, if they choose to do so, tax the group on its world-wide earnings rather than merely its local earnings?

On the basis of an empirical analysis of a sample of international firms, Hu concludes that 'these criteria usually produce an unambiguous answer: that it is a national corporation with international operations (i.e. foreign subsidiaries)' (p. 121).

Activity 1 _____

Examine your own organization in terms of the above criteria. What conclusion do you reach about the organization's international identity?

1. USA / CHINA (ASIA)
2. REGIONAL HQIS (e.g. B.U.)
   But all onto INC. (USA)
3. US/ Local — Europe have
   VP Finance & IT.
   GM UK
4. US
5. US

Comment

The bulk of The Open University's assets and people are located in the UK; local subsidiaries are, in most cases, UK controlled. The exception here is the activities of the Open University Business School in Central Europe where locally owned partners operate under licence to the School. Executive posts within the School are all held by UK nationals, while the Central European partners are nationals of the host country. The legal nationality of the OU is British, and it is to UK diplomats we would turn for political support and protection. We would be taxed (were we a profit-making body) under the laws of the UK. Thus, according to Hu, we are a national corporation with international operations.

International firms are *not* placeless. Neither are they all the same. Although, as profit-seeking enterprises operating within a capitalist market system, they do indeed share some common characteristics, they are far from being homogeneous. One of the most important causes of continuing differentiation among the population of international enterprises is the influence of the firm's *home environment* and its particular assemblage of political, economic, social and cultural attributes. In this respect, both the national and the local environment (as shown in Figure 1) are significant.

All international firms have an identifiable home base, which ensures that every company is essentially embedded within its domestic environment. Of course, the more extensive a firm's international operations the more likely it will be to take on additional characteristics from the host countries in which it operates. But home country characteristics are likely to remain the more dominant in most, if not all, cases. Despite many decades of operation as an international enterprise, therefore, Ford is still essentially a US company, ICI a British company and Siemens a German company.

A recent detailed study of United States, Japanese and German TNCs by Pauly and Reich (1997) provides additional evidence of the persistence of nationally-based differences. Focusing on such criteria as systems of corporate governance and financing, research and development strategies, foreign investment and intra-firm trade practices they find

> ... little blurring or convergence at the cores of firms based in Germany, Japan, or the United States ... Durable national institutions and distinctive ideological traditions still seem to shape and channel crucial corporate decisions ... there remain systematic and important national differences in the operations of [TNCs] – in their internal governance and long-term financing, in their R & D activities, and in their intertwined investment and trading strategies ... the domestic structures within which a firm initially develops leave a permanent imprint on its strategic behavior. At a time when many observers emphasize the importance of cross-border strategic alliances, regional business networks, and stock offerings on foreign exchanges – all suggestive of a blurring of corporate nationalities – our findings underline, for example, the durability of German financial control systems, the historical drive behind Japanese technology development through tight corporate networks, and the very different time horizons that lie behind American, German, and Japanese corporate planning.

(Pauly and Reich, 1997, pp. 1, 4, 5, 24)

The nation state is, in effect, the primary 'container' of distinctive social, political, economic and cultural institutions and practices. The particular attributes of each of these in combination contributes very strongly to the resultant nature of firms that originate there. Of course, we need to be careful about lapsing into simplistic 'environmental determinism' and of repeating the same error that the 'placeless' school of international business perpetrates on the global scale. Clearly, not all firms from the same domestic environment will be identical; the roles of individuals and specific corporate cultures developed over time will produce differences between firms of the same nationality. Ford and General Motors, for example, are both US automobile manufacturers, yet they are far from being identical. But the point is that there are likely to be greater inter-national differences than intra-national differences in the behaviour of firms.

Other units in this course focus upon specific aspects of culture, government and economics. Here I want to emphasize the importance of the particular *assemblage* of institutional components that are likely to mould domestic businesses and affect their international nature. Here the work of Whitley is especially useful. Whitley has made comparative studies of business systems in different countries both in Europe and in East Asia. He defines business systems as:

> ... particular arrangements of hierarchy–market relations which become institutionalised and relatively successful in particular contexts. They combine differences in the kinds of economic activities and skills which are authoritatively coordinated in firms, as opposed to being coordinated through market contracting, with variations in market organisation and differences in how activities are authoritatively directed. These differences can be seen as alternative responses to three fundamental issues in all market economies. First, how are economic activities and resources to be coordinated and controlled? Second, how are market connections between authoritatively coordinated economic activities in firms to be organised? Third, how are activities and skills within firms to be organised and directed through authority relations? The ways in which each of these issues is dealt with in different institutional contexts are, of course, interdependent and together constitute distinctive configurations of hierarchy–market relations in those contexts.

(Whitley, 1992a, p. 6)

Table 3 presents the major characteristics of business systems as defined by Whitley. It lists the three broad components which, together, constitute a distinctive business system: the nature of the firm, market organization, authoritative co-ordination and control systems.

Table 3   Characteristics of national business systems

1   The nature of the firm

- The degree to which private managerial hierarchies coordinate economic activities
- The degree of managerial discretion from owners
- Specialization of managerial capabilities and activities within authority hierarchies
- The degree to which growth is discontinuous and involves radical changes in skills and activities
- The extent to which risks are managed through mutual dependence with business partners and employees

2   Market organisation

- The extent of long-term cooperative relations between firms within and between sectors
- The significance of intermediaries in the coordination of market transaction
- Stability, integration and scope of business groups
- Dependence of cooperative relations on personal ties and trust

3   Authoritative coordination and control systems

- Integration and interdependence of economic activities
- Impersonality of authority and subordination relations
- Task, skill and role specialization and individualization
- Differentiation of authority roles and expertise
- Decentralization of operational control and level of work group autonomy
- Distance and superiority of managers
- Extent of employer–employee commitment and organization-based employment system

(Source: Whitley, 1992a, p. 9)

In sum, business systems are distinctive configurations of hierarchy–market relations which become institutionalized as relatively successful ways of organizing economic activities in different institutional environments. Certain kinds of activities are co-ordinated through particular sorts of authority structures and interconnected in different ways through various quasi-contractual arrangements in each business system. Thus, what resources are organized by differently structured hierarchies and markets varies between these systems, as do preferred ways of developing businesses and making choices. They develop and change in relation to dominant social institutions, especially those important during processes of industrialization. *The coherence and stability of these institutions, together with their dissimilarity between nation states, determine the extent to which business systems are distinctive, integrated and nationally differentiated.*

(Whitley, 1992b, p. 13, emphasis added)

Dunning (1979), whose Eclectic Paradigm of FDI you have seen before, provides some examples of the ways in which specific country characteristics may be translated into what he calls 'ownership-specific advantages'. As Table 4 (overleaf) shows, Dunning's scheme also incorporates what might be regarded as more traditional geographical factors, such as natural resource endowment, labour supply, market size and the like. But the message is the same: differences in the *specific assemblage* of characteristics contained within the national boundaries of nation states are reflected in differences in the nature of their business enterprises, and help to explain, for example, why Japanese firms are different from US firms, why British firms are different from German or French firms, and so on.

Table 4 Country-specific characteristics of business firms	
Ownership-specific advantages	**Country characteristics favouring such advantages**
1 Size of firm (e.g. economies of scale, product diversification)	Large and standardized markets. Liberal attitude towards mergers, conglomerates, industrial concentration
2 Management and organizational expertise	Availability of managerial manpower; educational and training facilities (e.g. business schools). Size of markets, etc. making for (1) above. Good R & D [research and development] facilities
3 Technological-based advantages	Government support of innovation. Availability of skilled [personnel] and in some cases of local materials
4 Labour and/or mature, small-scale intensive technologies	Plentiful labour supplies; good technicians. Expertise of small-firm/consultancy operation
5 Product differentiation, marketing economies	National markets with reasonably high incomes; high income elasticity of demand. Acceptance of advertising and other persuasive marketing methods. Consumer tastes and culture
6 Access to (domestic) markets	Large markets. No government control on imports. Liberal attitude to exclusive dealing
7 Access to, or knowledge about, natural resources	Local availability of resources encourages export of that knowledge and/or processing activities. Need for raw materials not available locally for domestic industry. Accumulated experience of expertise required for resource exploitation/processing
8 Capital availability and financial expertise	Good and reliable capital markets and professional advice
9 As it affects various advantages above	Role of government intervention and relationship with enterprises. Incentives to create advantages

(Based on Dunning, 1979, Table 6)

You will also remember that Porter (1990) provides a similar argument. Porter emphasizes a point which economic geographers have been making for many years: that *geographically localized concentrations* of economic activity are, themselves, extremely important in shaping the nature of the firms within them and, in Porter's terms, enhancing competitive advantage. This is the third geographical scale – local – in Figure 1.

1.4 CONCLUSION

This section has outlined the major geographical trends in the origins and destinations of international business and emphasized the importance of the characteristics of the home country environment to the nature of international business.

FDI has continued to grow at a very rapid rate which, since the mid-1980s in particular, has outpaced the growth of international trade. Such divergence in growth rates suggests that it is international *investment* by transnational corporations, rather than merely international trade, which is now the major integrating force in the global economy. However, the bulk of world FDI is contained within, or flows between, the three major components of the global triad, with only a relatively small proportion of FDI going to developing countries. But while this highly concentrated pattern continues to be reinforced by a dense network of cross-investment between the developed economies and by flows to a small number of developing countries, we are also beginning to see the emergence of significant outward flows of FDI from some newly industrializing economies, particularly in East Asia and Latin America.

The nature and characteristics of home country environments continue to exert an influence on the operations and behaviour of international firms. Such firms are certainly not 'placeless', as some writers have suggested.

2 THE GEOGRAPHICAL ORGANIZATION AND REORGANIZATION OF INTERNATIONAL ENTERPRISE

So far I have been concerned with the general influence of geography on the nature of international business and on the broad aggregate patterns of FDI. Now I shall turn to the question of how international firms organize themselves geographically and how geography influences the relationships between firms. I shall begin by examining what can be regarded as the basic building block: the production chain.

2.1 THE PRODUCTION (VALUE) CHAIN

The production of any good or service can be pictured as a chain of distinctive, although interlinked, functions. Figure 17 in the *Technology* unit presents one version (by Porter). It consists of a *transactionally linked* sequence of functions in which each stage in the sequence adds value to the process of production, whether of goods or services. For this reason, some writers use the term *value-added* chain (Johnston and Lawrence, 1988) or, more simply, *value chain* (Porter, 1986). Common to the entire chain of transactionally linked functions are the *technological processes* involved in production itself and in the physical movement of the constituent elements.

At one extreme, each function in the chain may be performed by individual independent firms so that the links in the chain consist of a series of external transactions between separate firms. In other words, transactions are organized through 'the market'. At the other extreme, the whole chain may be contained within a single firm. In this case, the links in the chain consist of a series of internal transactions within a particular firm. Here, transactions are organized hierarchically through the firm's internal organizational structure. Of course, these two organizational extremes of *markets* and *hierarchies* do not encompass the full range of possibilities. There are other forms of inter-unit co-ordination and collaboration which are increasingly significant.

The key issue here is that *different functions in the chain may be located in different places.* Geographically, the various components of the chain may be concentrated in particular places or dispersed. On an international or global scale, the extent to which this occurs, and the specific geographical organization of the production chain itself, depends primarily upon three factors:

1 the prevailing *technologies* of transport and communication as well as of production processes

2 the specific *strategic orientation* of the firm

3   the nature of the *political environment* which may create both
    constraints upon, and opportunities for, geographical concentration or
    dispersal of production chain functions.

2.2   THE INFLUENCE OF TECHNOLOGY ON THE GEOGRAPHY OF PRODUCTION CHAINS

Some particular aspects of technology are discussed in detail in the
Technology unit. Here, the focus is rather different.

A fundamental prerequisite for international business is the availability of
technologies that overcome the constraints of space and time. The most
important of such enabling technologies are those of *transport* and
communication – what we might term the space-shrinking technologies.
Both the geographical and the organizational scale on which any human
activity can occur is directly related to the available media of transport
and communication. Similarly, the degree of possible specialization is also
greatly influenced by these media. Transport systems are the means by
which materials, products, and other tangible entities (including, of
course, people) are transferred from place to place. Communications
systems are the means by which information is transmitted from place to
place in the form of instructions, orders, ideas, images and so on. For
most of human history, transport and communications were effectively
one and the same. Before the introduction of electric technology in the
nineteenth century, information could move only at the same speed, and
over the same distance, as the prevailing transport system would allow.
Electric technology broke that link, making it increasingly necessary to
treat transport and communication as separate, although intimately
related, technologies.

Developments in both transport and communications have dramatically
transformed our world, permitting unprecedented mobility of materials,
products, information and people. As Figure 5 (overleaf) shows, there is
no doubt that we live in a shrinking world. Both the *time* and *relative cost*
of transporting materials, products and people have fallen dramatically as
the result of a series of revolutionary and incremental technological
developments. Even more-far-reaching developments have occurred in
communications technology. Indeed, communications and information
technologies should now be regarded as the key technologies which are
transforming relationships at the global level:

> The new telecommunications technologies are the electronic highways
> of the informational age, equivalent to the role played by railway
> systems in the process of industrialization.

> *(Henderson and Castells, 1987, p. 6)*

Global communications systems have been transformed almost beyond
recognition during the past two or three decades through the introduction
of a range of significant innovations in information technology. The
essence of these developments, as shown in the Technology unit, is the
convergence between two specific technologies: communications and
computers.

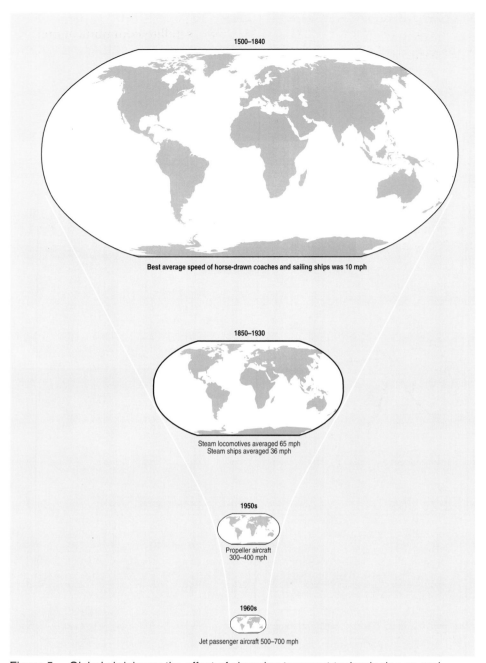

Figure 5   Global shrinkage: the effect of changing transport technologies on real distance (Dicken, 1998, Figure 5.3, p. 152)

These technologies are making possible unprecedented levels of global communication – both the sending of conventional messages and the transmission of computer data. It has become possible for a message to be transmitted in one location and received in another on the other side of the world virtually simultaneously. Until recently, the major creator of such capability was the *geo-stationary satellite* which, for the first time, meant that:

> ... communications costs are becoming insensitive to distance ... Within the beam of a satellite it makes no difference to costs whether you are transmitting for 500 miles or 5000 miles. The message goes up 22,300 miles to the satellite and down again 22,300 miles. It makes no difference whether the two points on earth are close together or far apart ... The important point about satellites is that their existence sets a limit on the extent to which costs are a function of distance.

(de Sola Pool, 1981, pp. 162–3)

Not only are satellite transmission costs insensitive to distance, but also user costs have fallen dramatically. However, satellite communications are now being challenged by *optical fibre* technologies. Optical fibre cable systems have a huge carrying capacity, and transmit information at very high speed and with a high signal strength. 'Each hair-like strand can now accommodate up to 60,000 simultaneous telephone calls (as opposed to 6–7,000 for a much wider coaxial cable)' (Graham and Marvin, 1996, p. 18).

Figure 6 shows the rapid increase in satellite and cable capacity in the Atlantic and Pacific regions, together with the basic skeleton of the optical fibre communications system being constructed in the Pacific and the more comprehensive plans to build a 'global digital highway'. This will link the world's three major markets of North America, Western Europe and Japan, using a network of optical fibre cables capable of carrying 100,000 simultaneous messages.

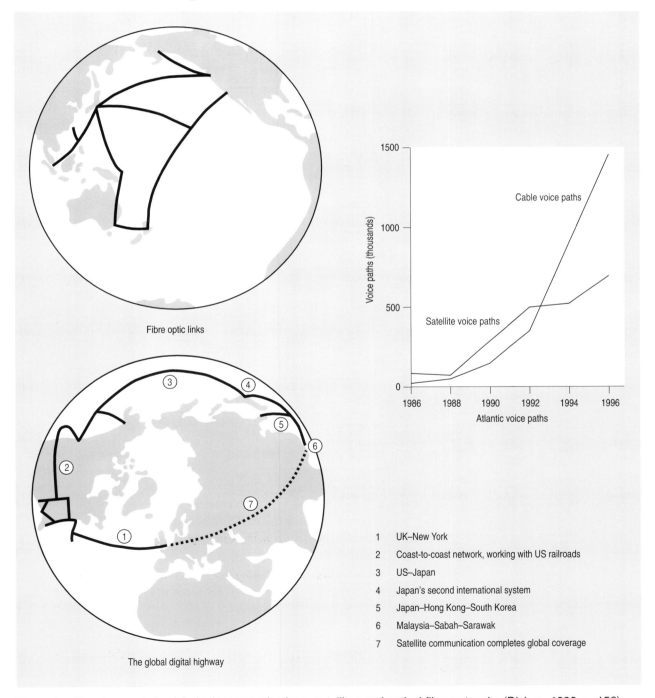

Fibre optic links

The global digital highway

1   UK–New York
2   Coast-to-coast network, working with US railroads
3   US–Japan
4   Japan's second international system
5   Japan–Hong Kong–South Korea
6   Malaysia–Sabah–Sarawak
7   Satellite communication completes global coverage

Figure 6   Developments in global telecommunications, satellites and optical fibre networks (Dicken, 1998, p. 156)

One result of all these developments has been a sharp decline in the cost of telecommunications services. Even so, the cost of international telecommunications remains far higher than should be the case in purely technological terms. This is because the telecommuications industry has been very highly regulated at the national scale, despite the moves towards deregulation in some parts of the world. Early in 1997, however, the World Trade Organization engineered an agreement to liberalize global telecommunications markets, which will greatly intensify competition as formerly protected national markets are opened up to the entry of foreign companies.

Review Question 1

Does the shrinking of geographical distance make geography less or more important from a business viewpoint? In other words, do the characteristics of particular places still exert an influence on business decision making or are all places equally likely to attract investment?

Developments in transport and communications – the space-shrinking technologies – are the most obvious influence changing the ways in which international firms may organize and configure their production chains. Less obvious, but highly significant, are developments in *production process technologies*. Most significant at the present time are the technologies that facilitate greater *flexibility* in the production process itself and in the organization of relationships between customers and suppliers. One key to production flexibility is the use of *information technologies* in machines and operations. These permit more sophisticated control over the production process. With the increasing sophistication of automated processes and, especially, the new flexibility of electronically controlled technology, far-reaching changes in the process of production need not necessarily be associated with increased scale of production. Indeed, one of the major results of the new electronic and computer-aided production technology is that it permits rapid switching from one part of a process to another and allows the more precise tailoring of production to customer requirements.

At present, therefore, there appears to be a diversity of production processes. On the one hand, we can observe trends towards:

- an increasingly finer degree of specialization in many production processes, enabling their *fragmentation* into a number of discrete operations, and
- an increasing *standardization and routinization* of these individual operations, enabling the use of semi-skilled and unskilled labour; this is especially apparent in the mature stage of a product's life-cycle.

On the other hand, we can also identify a clear trend towards:

- an increasing *flexibility* in the production process, which is altering the old relationship between the scale and the cost of production, permitting smaller production runs, increasing product variety, and changing the ways in which production and the labour process are organized.

Developments in the space-shrinking technologies and in new technologies of production increase the options for firms to separate out parts of their production chain and to locate them in the most advantageous places, either to minimize costs or to increase revenues. However, it is not just technology that determines the precise outcomes:

the interactions between the strategic orientation of the firm and the policies of governments are especially significant.

2.3   THE STRATEGIC ORIENTATION OF THE INTERNATIONAL FIRM

Different strategic orientations will place different requirements on how a firm's production chain is organized and geographically configured.

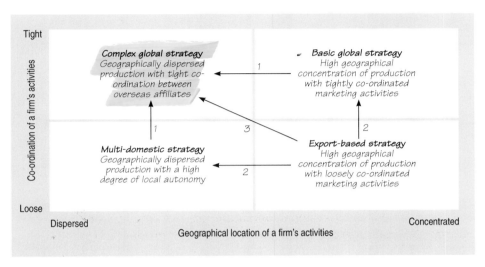

Figure 7   A typology of international competitive strategies (Dicken, 1992, p. 195; adapted in part from Porter, 1986, p. 28)

Figure 7 shows four general types of international competitive strategy arranged according to two primary axes – co-ordination of a firm's activities on the vertical axis and geographical location on the horizontal axis – and three possible routes to the option complex global strategy. Each of the four strategies involves different degrees of geographical concentration or dispersal of value-added activities. Two of the options – the export-based strategy and the basic global strategy – involve a high degree of geographical concentration of production activities. The other two options – the multi-domestic strategy and the complex global strategy – involve a high degree of geographical dispersion. However, the organizational co-ordination decision and the geographical location decision have to be made for each element in the firm's production or value-added chain. Some elements may be geographically dispersed; other elements may be geographically concentrated. Some elements of the chain may be located in close geographical proximity to one another, whereas others may be separately located:

> A firm may standardize (concentrate) some activities and tailor (disperse) others. It may also be able to standardize and tailor at the same time through the coordination of dispersed activities, or use local tailoring of some activities (e.g., different product positioning in each country) to allow standardization of others (e.g., production).

> *(Porter, 1986, p. 35)*

In fact, combining standardization and local tailoring is becoming increasingly possible with the emergence of flexible production technology. *The tendency to dichotomize corporate competitive strategies into global versus national, cost versus differentiation, concentration versus dispersal, is clearly a gross oversimplification:*

> [Firms] must balance pressures for integrating globally with those for responding idiosyncratically to national environments ... [however] ... there may not be a single optimal point on the fragmentation–unification continuum but a range of tenable positions.

(Kobrin, 1988, pp. 104, 107)

2.4 THE POLITICAL ENVIRONMENT

The precise way in which an international firm organizes its production chain activities – its internal division of labour or degree of geographical specialization – is clearly influenced by the interplay between technology and strategic orientation. However, the *nature of the political environment* is also a significant influence on the firm's geography in so far as national boundaries are 'containers' of a set of location-specific factors (including markets, labour supplies, and resources). In the Government unit, the detailed nature of the political environment facing international firms is discussed. Here, we need merely to remind ourselves that the existence of political boundaries creates major 'discontinuities' on the surface of international activity. Such discontinuities present both constraints and opportunities to international firms as they attempt to implement their specific strategies. For example, a firm may wish to implement a comprehensive global strategy involving an intricate world-wide geographical configuration of its production chain activities by locating each part in its optimal location. Both the transport and communications and the production technologies may be in place to facilitate the strategy. However, the extent to which the strategy can be implemented in practice may well be limited by different regulations in different countries which control access to markets and resources.

Whether or not a specific national regulation is a constraint or an opportunity to a firm will depend, at least in part, on whether the firm is pursuing a nationally responsive or a globally integrated strategy. For example, the primary requirement for a firm pursuing a nationally responsive strategy is unhindered access to its target markets. Regulatory barriers, such as tariff or non-tariff barriers, will usually influence a firm's decision to set up operations within the regulated market. The picture is complicated in regional economic groupings, such as the European Community before the completion of the Single European Market, where there are different regulatory barriers affecting a firm's geographical strategy but where access to the larger regional market may be achieved. In these circumstances, firms may well be able to play off one member country against another on the basis of intra-regional differences in regulations.

A more complex situation arises in the case of firms attempting to pursue a globally integrated strategy. The essence of such a strategy is the ability to locate each part of the production chain in optimal conditions (for example, to use cheap labour for basic assembly operations). The integrated structure, therefore, consists of a complex network of managerial, research, production, marketing, distribution and service nodes linked together by intricate cross-border flows. On the one hand, such global networks provide firms with the potential ability to minimize regulatory constraints and maximize regulatory opportunities because they may be able to switch and reswitch their operations between alternative locations. In this sense, international firms may be able to engage in 'regulatory arbitrage', that is, to benefit from the different regulations in different countries. Most obviously this is the case with transfer pricing. More generally, however, the ability to engage in regulatory arbitrage is limited by the existence of fixed capital investments. On the other hand, states may well have the ability to inhibit the achievement of a globally integrated strategy. As Doz has argued:

> ... host governments wield the power to limit the extent of, or even to dismantle, the MNC [multinational corporation] integrated manufacturing and trade network with more regulations and restrictions on foreign investments and market access.

> *(Doz, 1986, p. 39)*

In such circumstances, what matters is the relative bargaining power of the firm on the one hand and the state on the other.

Review Question 2

Which kinds of government policy are most likely to affect a firm's ability to implement a global strategy?

2.5   THE INTERNAL GEOGRAPHY OF THE INTERNATIONAL FIRM

It should now be clear that the internal geographical division of labour in a particular international firm is the result of a complex interaction between three sets of processes:

- the strategic orientation of the firm itself
- the nature of the prevailing technologies in the industry in question
- the regulatory/political environment which determines access to markets and resources.

The problem is that different parts of an international enterprise have different locational needs which can be satisfied by various types of geographical location. Each part tends, therefore, to develop rather distinctive geographical patterns.

This can be illustrated by looking in turn at four of the most important functions in an international enterprise: corporate and regional headquarters offices, R & D facilities, production units, and services. Each of these, as you will see, displays certain geographical regularities, notably a highly uneven pattern of distribution both globally and locally. Other functions such as marketing and sales, or distribution and service, tend to be distributed far more widely in accordance with the firm's geographical markets. Indeed, as competition intensifies, firms are increasingly placing an emphasis on the service component of their business (which involves investment in marketing, local distribution channels and the like). This is as true in industrial products as in consumer products, and is spreading rapidly through many industries. A local market presence is becoming essential.

Corporate and regional headquarters

The corporate headquarters is the locus of overall control. Its staff are concerned with making the high-level strategic decisions that shape and direct the whole enterprise – which products and markets to enter or to leave, whether to expand or contract particular parts of the enterprise, whether to acquire other firms or to sell off existing parts. It is concerned, then, with all the major investment and disinvestment decisions. One of its most important roles is financial: it is the corporate headquarters which holds the purse strings and which decides on the level and allocation of the corporate budget between the component units. In the global corporation the horizons of the corporate headquarters are global and its time-span tends to be long-term rather than short-term. Headquarters offices are, above all, handlers, processors, and transmitters and receivers of information to and from other parts of the enterprise and also between similarly high-level organizations outside. The most important of these are the major business services on which the corporation depends (financial, legal, advertising) and also, very often, major departments of government, both foreign and domestic.

Regional headquarters offices of international enterprises constitute an intermediate level in the corporate hierarchy. They usually have a broad geographical sphere of influence, which covers several countries, and perform a distinctive role in the internal affairs of the firm. Their major responsibility is to co-ordinate and control the activities of the firm's affiliates (manufacturing units, sales offices, etc.) and to act as intermediaries between the corporate headquarters and its affiliates within the region. Branch affiliates generally report to regional headquarters which, in turn, report to the corporate head office. Thus, the regional headquarters act as channels of communication, transmitting instructions from the corporate centre to its affiliates and information from the affiliates back to the centre. Regional headquarters will, of course, have their own decision-making responsibilities and may also perform a regional marketing function. Regional headquarters are both co-ordinating mechanisms within the firm and also an important part of its 'intelligence-gathering' system.

These characteristic functions of corporate and regional headquarters define their particular locational requirements. Both require a strategic location on the global transport and communications network in order to keep in close contact with other, geographically dispersed, parts of the organization. Both require access to high-quality external services and a particular range of labour market skills, especially people skilled in information processing. Since much corporate headquarters activity involves interaction with the head offices of other organizations, there are strong agglomerating forces involved. Face-to-face contacts with the top executives of other high-level organizations are facilitated by close geographical proximity. Such high-powered executives invariably prefer a location that is rich in social and cultural amenities.

At the global scale, only a relatively small number of cities contains a large proportion of both corporate and regional headquarters offices of TNCs. Such *global cities* are sometimes described as the geographical 'control points' of the global economy. Figure 8 presents a simplified map of these centres (the links shown are diagrammatic only; they are intended solely to give an impression of a connected network of cities). Three global cities – New York, Tokyo and London – stand head and shoulders above all the others. Below them is a tier of other key cities in each of the three major economic regions of the world – Western Europe, North America and Asia – with other representation in Australia and Latin America.

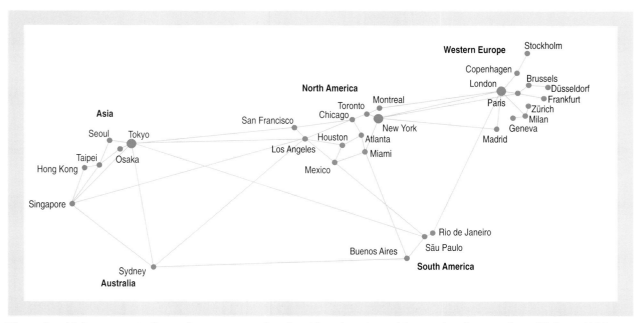

Figure 8   Major concentrations of corporate and regional headquarters of international enterprises (Dicken, 1998, p. 210; adapted in part from Friedmann, 1986, Figure 1 and Cohen, 1981, pp. 307–8)

One of the striking features of the geography of corporate headquarters is that very few, if any, major TNCs have moved their ultimate decision-making operations outside their home country (although the Swedish firm Ericsson was recently reported to be considering moving its corporate headquarters from Stockholm to London). This is one further indicator of the continuing significance of the home base. On the other hand, there is quite a lot of evidence of TNCs relocating major divisional headquarters overseas. For example, in the early 1990s, several major US companies, including IBM, Hewlett Packard and Monsanto, did exactly that as part of major corporate reorganization. In each case, however, there was no question of the overall headquarters function being relocated outside the United States.

Both the development of the single European market and the rapid growth of the East and South East Asian economies have stimulated the need for regional headquarters in those areas. United States TNCs, which have had a presence in Europe for a very long time, have been establishing European headquarters to co-ordinate their regional operations. A number of Japanese TNCs have set up regional headquarters in Europe as the scale and extent of Japanese operations within Europe have increased (Aoki and Tachiki, 1992). In Asia, the Singapore government introduced an Operational Headquarters Scheme which has attracted a considerable number of foreign TNCs to establish regional headquarters in Singapore (Dicken and Kirkpatrick, 1991).

Within individual countries, on the other hand, the locational pattern of both corporate and – especially – regional headquarters is far from static. Geographical decentralization of corporate headquarters out of the city centres of New York and London has certainly been occurring. In the case of London, most of these shifts are a short distance to the less congested outer reaches of the metropolitan area. In the United States, on the other hand, there appears to be a much higher degree of locational change in

GEOGRAPHY

headquarters functions. Detailed empirical research by Lyons and Salmon for the period 1974–1989 shows a considerable degree of change:

> Although the highest concentration of corporate headquarters continues to be found among the four diversified national metropolitan regions, New York, Chicago, Los Angeles and San Francisco (48.7 per cent of the top 250 in 1989), only Los Angeles recorded an increase in concentration. The majority of the declines were concentrated in New York (-11.5 per cent), although ... New York continues to be the most important centre of corporate headquarter locations. The major beneficiaries of New York's demise were a select group of smaller regional diversified cities ... in particular Atlanta, Dallas/Fort Worth, Philadelphia, and St Louis.

> *(Lyons and Salmon, 1995, pp. 103–4)*

Nevertheless, apart from the United States, the fact that the locational needs of corporate and regional headquarters of TNCs are satisfied most readily in the very large city means that they tend not to be spread very widely within any particular country. In the United Kingdom, for example, there are very few corporate headquarters of major firms or regional headquarters of foreign TNCs outside London and the South East; in France, few locate outside Paris. In Italy, the most important centre is Milan, in the highly industrialized north, which is more important than Rome as a location for foreign TNCs. Such strong geographical polarization is even more apparent in the developing countries.

Review Question 3

(a) Why do you think that face-to-face contacts continue to be important in the location of important decision-making functions of business firms?

(b) To what extent do you think that technology will displace such contacts in the near future?

Research and development facilities

In general, international firms spend more than other firms on R & D as part of their drive to remain competitive and profitable on a world scale. Innovation – of new products or new processes – is critically important for such firms in an increasingly competitive global economy. The R & D function is, therefore, highly significant for them. Indeed, it has become even more important with the intensified pace and changing nature of technology.

The process of R & D is a complex sequence of operations in which three phases can be identified. In phase 1 the emphasis is on applied science and marketing research, phase 2 is concerned with product design and development, while phase 3 is the 'debugging' of products and their adaptation to local circumstances. Each phase tends to have rather different locational requirements, although in each case the firm has to reconcile several factors. One is the advantage of scale economies derived from concentrating R & D against the need to locate R & D closer to other corporate functions or to markets. The primary need in phase 1 is for access to the basic sources of science and marketing information – universities, research institutes, trade associations, and so on. Phase 2 tends to require large-scale teamwork, that is, access to a sufficiently large supply of highly qualified scientists, engineers and technicians. Phase 3's locational requirements are for quick two-way contact with the users of the innovation: the production or marketing units themselves.

There are important differences in the type of R & D undertaken by international firms in their overseas locations. According to Behrman and Fischer (1980) the operation of each type of R & D activity varies according to the specific market orientation of the firm. They identify three groups of international firm: home market firms, host market firms, and world market firms. Each tends to have a rather different R & D pattern. Firms which have a strong home market orientation tend to carry out little overseas R & D, and that which is carried out is usually of the support laboratory type. Home market firms have tended to believe that their foreign sales do not require any further R & D beyond that carried out for their domestic market.

> 'Host market' international firms – those oriented towards the national (or regional) market in which their overseas operations are located – operate both support laboratories and also higher level locally integrated laboratories. The most important locational criteria are proximity to the firm's overseas markets and the fact that the firm's overseas operations are sufficiently substantial to justify separate R & D activities. Such activities tend to be located in the firm's biggest and most important overseas markets. 'World market' firms are the truly global corporations whose orientation is to world, rather than to national, markets. Their R & D activities may well include both support and locally integrated laboratories but their adoption of a globally integrated production strategy is leading them to establish specially designed international interdependent research laboratories.
>
> The major locational criteria for these world market R & D activities are the availability of highly skilled scientists and engineers, access to sources of basic scientific and technical developments and an appropriate infrastructure.
>
> Universities were frequently mentioned as an important means of gaining access to the foreign scientific and technical communities that are of such great interest to the foreign exploratory laboratories of world-market companies. Every one of the world-market firms stressed the need for a strong local university system as a prerequisite for choosing an overseas location for R & D.
>
> *(Behrman and Fischer, 1980, p. 21)*

Such stringent locational demands at present tend to limit these high-level R & D activities to a relatively small number of developed countries.

As in the case of their corporate headquarters, TNCs show a very strong preference for keeping their high-level R & D in their home countries. The United States Office of Technology Assessment (1994) calculated that only around 13 per cent of the total R & D performed by United States manufacturing TNCs is located abroad. In fact, most of the overseas R & D carried out by TNCs of all national origins has to do with the relatively low-level adaptation of existing products and processes to local conditions. Although there has been some geographical dispersal of R & D, its actual extent is the subject of some dispute. On the one hand, writers like Howells identify a substantial degree of R & D dispersal globally:

> As more companies move from being 'host market' to 'world market' firms, the role of R & D has moved from a direct but secondary role of helping to serve the market via product modification towards a much more integrated mechanism in gaining new markets. Increasingly the

sources of new ideas for new products and innovations are coming from the user firms and industries and if firms are to remain competitive and be able to move into new markets they must be able to maintain close relationships with their existing and potential customers.

(Howells, 1990, p. 504)

Howells also points to another important influence stimulating the geographical spread of R & D by TNCs: the growing demand for skilled scientists. This particular labour market is intensely competitive and is forcing firms to extend their R & D networks in order to capture geographically dispersed scientific workers.

Others, however, contest the extent to which there has been a really significant *general* shift in the international location of R & D. Detailed empirical analyses of patent data for almost 600 firms by Patel (1995) produced the following conclusions:

- only 43 firms in the sample (7.6%) located more than half of their technological activities outside their home country
- more than 40 per cent of the sample performed less than 1 per cent of their technological activity abroad
- more than 70 per cent of the sample performed less than 10 per cent of this activity abroad
- very little of the overseas R & D activity of firms from the United States, Japan, Germany, France and Italy is located outside the 'global triad'
- most of the apparent increases in overseas R & D came about through merger and acquisition rather than through internal growth and geographical expansion.

Why should such home-country bias in R & D persist? Why do TNCs show such a strong preference for keeping their major R & D activities close to their home base? Patel's explanation reflects the significance of geographical proximity:

> Two key features related to the launching of major innovations may help explain the advantages of geographic concentration: the involvement of inputs of knowledge and information that are essentially 'person-embodied', and a high degree of uncertainty surrounding outputs. Both of these are best handled through geographic concentration. Thus it may be most efficient for firms to concentrate the core of their technological activities in the home base with international 'listening posts' and small foreign laboratories for adaptive R & D.

(Patel, 1995, p. 152)

Not only are corporate R & D activities strongly concentrated in TNCs' home countries but also the spatial pattern *within* nations is very uneven. The support laboratories are the most widely spread in that they generally locate close to the production units, although not every production unit has an associated support laboratory. But the larger-scale R & D activities tend to be confined to particular kinds of location. Their need for a large supply of highly trained scientists, engineers and technicians, together with proximity to universities and other research institutions, confines them to large urban complexes, which are often also the location of the firm's corporate headquarters. A secondary locational influence is the 'quality of living' for the highly educated and highly paid research staff: an amenity-rich setting, including a good climate and potential for leisure activities as well as a stimulating intellectual environment, is desirable.

Spatial patterns of corporate R & D in both the USA and the UK illustrate both of these locational influences. In the USA, corporate R & D is still predominantly a big-city activity despite recent growth in smaller urban areas. The pull of the amenity-rich environment is illustrated by the considerable concentration of R & D activities in locations such as Los Angeles, San Francisco and San Diego in California, Denver-Boulder in Colorado and the 'research triangle' in North Carolina. In the UK, corporate R & D, like corporate headquarters and regional offices, is disproportionately concentrated in south-east England. Within this region firms can both be close to London with all its intellectual, social and cultural facilities and also locate in some of the 'green and pleasant' lands of the South East.

Production units

There are clearly some identifiable geographical regularities in the patterns of both corporate headquarters and R & D functions. This is because the locational needs of corporate offices and R & D laboratories are broadly similar for all firms, regardless of the particular industries in which they are involved. This is not so for production units. Consequently, it is far more difficult to generalize about their locational tendencies. Their locational requirements vary considerably depending upon the specific organizational and technological role they perform within the enterprise and the geographical distribution of the relevant location-specific factors. It is certainly true that, compared with corporate headquarters and R & D facilities, production units of TNCs have become more and more dispersed geographically. But there is no single and simple trend or pattern of dispersal common to all activities, whether at the global scale or within individual nations. The pattern varies greatly from one industry to another. Figure 9 (overleaf) illustrates diagrammatically four types of geographical orientation which a TNC might adopt for its production units.

Globally concentrated production

Figure 9(a) is the simplest case. Here it is assumed that the firm concentrates all its production at a single geographical location (or, at least, within a single country) and serves its world markets through its marketing and sales networks. This is a procedure consistent with the basic global strategy shown in the upper right cell of Figure 7. It is the kind of strategy followed by many Japanese companies until their relatively recent move towards more dispersed global production.

Host market production

Figure 9(b) depicts what has been, so far, the most common production strategy for international firms. Here production is located in, and oriented directly to, a specific host market. Where that market is similar in character to the firm's home market the product is likely to be identical to that produced at home. Such production units have been variously termed 'miniature replicas' of home country plants or 'relay affiliates'. In many cases, however, the product may have to be adapted to the circumstances of the local market, and R & D facilities may need to be established as well. The specific locational criteria for the setting up of host market plants are (fairly obviously): the size and sophistication of the

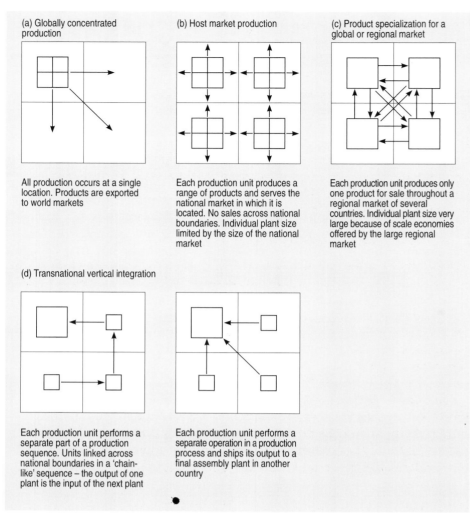

Figure 9 Some major ways of organizing the production units of international firms (Dicken, 1998, p. 215)

market as reflected in income levels; the structure of demand and consumer tastes; and the cost-related advantages of locating directly in the market. In effect, this kind of production is import substituting. Most of the manufacturing plants established by US firms in Europe in the post-1945 period were of this kind, in many cases following a product life-cycle sequence. The more recent surge of European manufacturing investment in the USA is also directly host market related. Similarly, the large markets of some developed countries, such as Brazil, have attracted considerable numbers of manufacturing affiliates of international enterprises whose role is to serve that market directly.

With the development of the various enabling technologies that have combined to shrink geographical distances, the establishment of a production unit in a specific geographical market becomes less necessary in purely cost terms. However, there are two reasons for the continued development of host market production. One is the need to be close to the market in order to be sensitive to variations in customer demands, tastes and preferences, or to be able to provide a rapid after-sales service. As I have noted already, sensitivity to local geographical differences continues to be an important issue even where firms pursue broadly global strategies for their overall business. The second factor influencing the continuation of host market production plants is political: the existence of tariff and, particularly, non-tariff barriers to trade.

Tariff barriers have been a significant locational factor from the very early days of international investment. In general, of course, tariffs have been falling as a result of the successive General Agreement on Tariffs and Trade (GATT) and WTO negotiations. Today it is the various kinds of non-tariff barrier – especially import quotas and 'voluntary trade agreements' – which have become the major feature of trade policy in many nations. Again, these have acted as a stimulus to firms to jump over the barriers and establish direct production units to serve the local market. There is no doubt, for example, that the recent growth of Japanese and other Asian manufacturing investment in Western Europe and in North America is substantially a response to the actual, or threatened, existence of non-tariff trade restrictions.

Product specialization for a global or regional market

Globally concentrated production and host market production are the longest-established forms of production orientation among international firms. However, during the last three decades or so, a radically different form of production organization has emerged: production as part of a rationalized product or process strategy. Figure 9(c) shows this kind of product specialization for a global or a large regional market (such as the European Union (EU) or North America). Many argue that such large specialized plants will become the norm after the completion of the Single European Market when all internal barriers to the movement of goods, services and factors of production are finally removed. In fact, there is likely to be considerable variation from industry to industry and also within industries, because the creation of a single market will not necessarily mean the creation of a uniform market in terms of tastes and preferences.

The industries involved in large-scale specialized production units in such regional markets as the EU or continental North America are quite varied, although rationalized production tends to be most common in particular sectors, notably the technologically more advanced sectors, the large-volume medium-technology consumer goods industries, and the mass-production industries supplying branded goods. The existence of a huge internal market, together with differences in factor endowments between member nations, facilitates the establishment of very large specialized units which serve the entire regional market rather than single national markets. The key locational consideration, therefore, is the 'trade-off' between the economies of large-scale production at one or a small number of large plants and the additional transport costs involved in assembling the necessary inputs and in shipping the final product to a geographically extensive regional market.

Transnational vertical integration of production

The other kind of rationalized production strategy involves geographical specialization by process or by semi-finished product (Figure 9(d)). As I noted in Section 2.2, technological innovations in the production process permit a number of processes to be fragmented into separate parts and have led to a greater degree of standardization in some manufacturing operations. Parallel developments in transport and communications technology and in organizational technology have introduced a much enhanced flexibility into the geographical location of the production process. It has become possible for firms to locate some of their production units to take advantage of geographical variations in production costs on a global scale, notably in developing countries. Thus, transnational vertical integration becomes feasible whereby different parts of a firm's production system are located in different parts of the world. Materials, semi-finished products, components and finished products are transported between the geographically dispersed production units.

In these circumstances there may be no direct link at all between the location of production itself and the national market in which the production unit is located. The traditional market connection is broken. The output of a manufacturing plant in one country may simply be the input for a plant belonging to the same firm located in another country. Alternatively, the finished product may be exported to a third-country market or to the home market of the parent firm. In these circumstances the term 'export platform' is used to describe the role of the country in which production is located. The plants themselves are sometimes termed 'workshop affiliates'; their role is to act as international sourcing points for the international firm as a whole. Hence, the process is often called 'offshore,' or 'international intra-firm', sourcing. Figure 9(d) shows two simplified ways in which such international process specialization might be organized as part of a vertically integrated set of operations across national boundaries.

Offshore sourcing and the development of vertically integrated production networks on a global scale were virtually unknown before the early 1960s. The pioneers were US firms (notably in electronics), which set up offshore assembly operations in East and South-East Asia as well as in Mexico, followed later by some European and Japanese firms. The growth of such international production networks was extremely rapid during the late 1960s and throughout the 1970s. If anything, the world recession of the 1970s intensified the search for low-cost production locations in order for firms to remain competitive and maintain profitability. But it is important to stress that not all industries or processes are suitable for offshore sourcing.

The activities involved tend to be in two broad groups. First, there are those products at the mature stage of the product life-cycle in which the technology has become standardized, long production runs are needed, and semi-skilled or unskilled labour costs are very important. Second, there are certain parts of the production process of newer industries which are also labour-intensive and amenable to the employment of semi-skilled and unskilled labour even though the industry as a whole is highly capital- and technology-intensive.

International intra-firm sourcing – the setting up by international firms of production units in developing countries – has become an increasingly important mechanism in the global integration of production processes in which:

> ... the more mobile factors, such as technology, management and equipment, are moved to the site of the least mobile. Through this method the multinational corporation is able to utilize the labour of the less developed countries in production processes formerly associated only with the more industrialized. It brings together both low-cost labour and advanced techniques.

> *(Leontiades, 1971, p. 27)*

However, the choice of location for a production unit on the global scale is by no means as simple as it is often made out to be. It is not just a matter of looking at differences in labour costs between one country and another or at the incentives offered as part of an export-oriented policy.

Despite the enormous shrinkage of geographical distance that has occurred, the relative geographical location of parent company and overseas production unit may still be significant. If it were not for the influence of distance (broadly defined) we might expect the offshore production plants to be drawn to locations with the lowest labour costs. Yet this is not so. The sheer organizational convenience of geographical proximity may encourage firms to locate offshore production close to their home country even when labour costs there are higher than elsewhere. A clear example of this is Mexico in the case of US firms and parts of Southern Europe in the case of European firms. Although labour costs are indeed relatively low in both Mexico and Southern Europe they are not as low as in many other parts of the world. The advantage of these locations is geographical proximity.

Of course, just as geographical proximity may override differentials in labour costs, so too other locational influences may dominate in any particular case. Not all offshore sourcing arrangements are regional in nature. For the largest international firms – the global corporations – the world is indeed their oyster. Their production units are spread globally, often as part of a strategy of dual or multiple sourcing of components or products. This is one way of avoiding the risk of reliance on a single source whose operations may be disrupted for a variety of reasons. In a vertically integrated production sequence in which individual production units are tightly interconnected, an interruption in supply can seriously affect the other units, perhaps those located on the other side of the world. In an extreme case, a whole segment of a firm's operations may be halted.

Services

So far, the discussion of locational issues has primarily related to the production of tangible goods. But the growth in the internationalization of services has (some believe) outstripped the growth in the internationalization of production.

The services sector is extremely diverse – far more so, in many respects, than the manufacturing sector. It ranges from the highly sophisticated knowledge- and information-intensive activities performed in both private and public sector organizations to the very basic services of cleaning and simple maintenance. It includes retail and wholesale distribution and entertainment as well as health care and education services. It encompasses construction activities, transport activities, financial activities, communications activities and professional services. The list is (almost) endless.

As the services sector has become an increasingly significant element in economies, it has been common to classify services as either *consumer* services, or *producer* (or business) services. But such a classification is not always as fruitful as it might seem. Most services are '*mixed*' in that they are both producer and consumer services. Obvious examples are transportation and communication services, hotels, and many financial services.

In contrast to the producer/consumer categorization, I would suggest using the notion of the production chain (introduced in Section 2.1) to help understand the role of services in an economy. Figure 10 (overleaf) shows that service inputs are needed at each stage of the production

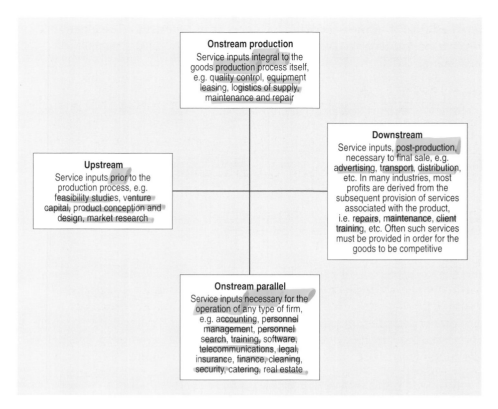

Figure 10   The interconnections between services and production in the production chain (adapted from UNCTC, 1988, p. 177)

process. It also shows an increasingly significant aspect of today's competitive environment:

> ... services have become a major source of value-added. Downstream services in particular are both a factor contributing to competitive strength and a source of value-added.
>
> (UNCTC, 1988, p. 178)

But the value of services to the competitiveness of products is more general than this and applies throughout the production chain:

> In a number of product markets it is the 'services' ... design, styling, research, marketing, delivery, packaging, consumer credit – which determine the competitiveness of agricultural and manufacturing investment. As the length of production chains increases, so services are responsible for a greater share of value added to products.
>
> (Britton, 1990, p. 538)

In other words,

> Service activities not only provide linkages between the segments of production within a [production chain] and linkages between overlapping [production chains], but they also bind together the spheres of production and circulation. Services have come to play a critical role in [production chains] because they not only provide geographical and transactional connections, but they *integrate* and *coordinate* the atomized and globalized production process.
>
> (Raback and Kim, 1994, p.123)

The internationalization of most economic activity generally occurs via two means. One way is through international trade; the other is through some kind of presence in a particular overseas location or market.

Services clearly fit the second form: firms may establish a presence in a foreign market to provide their services to local or locally based customers.

But are services *tradable*? Many are not because they need to be consumed at the point of production; they are not storable. It is possible that 'information-based services' mediated by increasingly sophisticated telecommunications and electronic data exchange can flow between geographically separated producers and consumers. Nevertheless, the supplying firm usually needs to have an actual presence in the foreign market to deliver the service more efficiently and effectively.

Thus the real issue in the location of service industries is the conditions under which providers of services establish a presence in a specific national market. In short, the debate reduces to the question of FDI and the other modes of international involvement that firms may use.

For many service industries, particularly those which are primarily intermediate inputs into the production chain and those which are circulation activities (for example financial and commercial services), the initial stimulus to their internationalization was the rapid growth and global spread of international enterprises in manufacturing industries. In many respects, the internationalization both of manufacturing and these business service activities has become mutually reinforcing.

Activity 2 _____

Identify the major locational requirements of the production units in your organization or an organization with which you are familiar. Consider how these relate to the four types of international production discussed in this section.

Comment _____

First of all, I have defined the Open University Business School as a service organization. Now, I've heard it said that in some ways the OU is a production organization like a publishing house. This, in fact, fits with the discussion immediately above. Our corporate headquarters, R & D, and our production of English language materials are all located in or around Milton Keynes, although translated versions of some of the course material are produced in Central Europe. To that extent, our production is primarily globally concentrated, with elements of host country production.

But, as I said, we are a service organization and therefore, because of the nature of services, we are also required to deliver services where they are consumed. To that extent, we attempt to provide tutors and other services wherever there are significant concentrations of students.

2.6 THE EXTERNAL GEOGRAPHY OF THE INTERNATIONAL FIRM

So far I have concentrated upon the geographical dimensions of the *internal* relationships between the constituent parts of international firms. But, although such firms, by definition, operate complex internal networks of relationships, they are also locked into *external networks* of relationships with a myriad of other firms. Such inter-firm relationships constitute the 'external geography' of the firm. Many of the attributes of this geography are similar to those discussed in the previous section. In this section I focus upon one aspect of the highly complex subject of inter-firm relationships: the geographical dimension of the relationships between customers for, and suppliers of, materials, components, semi-finished products and the broad range of business services. Although such inputs are frequently procured 'in-house' from within the firm's own branches and subsidiaries, not even the most highly integrated firm is totally self-sufficient. All firms acquire at least some of their inputs from outside suppliers. Indeed, possibly between 50 and 70 per cent of manufacturing costs are spent on purchased inputs. Some of these purchases will be, as it were, 'off-the-shelf' or 'catalogue' sourcing from independent suppliers at the arm's-length market price. However, a significant proportion – perhaps the majority – of such purchases are made through the formal mechanism of subcontracting, which is a kind of half-way house between complete internalization of procurement and arm's-length transactions on the open market.

The geographical dimension of subcontracting

As a process, subcontracting is as old as industrialization itself, if not older. The 'putting-out' system was a key element of most industries from their earliest stages. It depended, essentially, on close geographical proximity between firms and their subcontractors. The very fine and intricate network of subcontracting relationships based on the externalization of transactions in the production chain often led to the development of highly localized industrial districts. Such tight, functionally and transactionally based, geographical agglomerations of linked economic activities declined in most Western industrial countries with increasing speed between the 1960s and early 1980s, although they persisted in Japan.

Indeed, Japan still has one of the most highly developed domestic subcontracting networks. Each large Japanese firm is surrounded by a constellation of small and medium-sized subcontracting firms, which act as suppliers of components or perform specialist processes to the specification, and the timetable, laid down by the controlling large firm. Indeed, the Japanese subcontracting system, with its sharp distinction between the two major segments, has contributed a great deal to the international competitiveness of the Japanese economy. Competitiveness within the subcontracting segment is fierce; the supplier firms are very heavily subservient to the stringent demands of the principal companies.

One of the most significant developments of the last 30 years has been the extension of subcontracting across national boundaries: the emergence of *international subcontracting* as an important global activity. The revolution in transport and communications technology, together with developments in the production process itself, has created the potential for firms to establish subcontracting networks over vast geographical distances in the same way as international firms have established offshore production units of their own (see Section 2.5). Relatively low transportation costs, plus the ability to control and co-ordinate the operation of a long-distance subcontracting system, have allowed firms to take advantage of very low labour costs in developing countries.

The changing relationship between customers and suppliers

A major incentive for international firms to engage in international subcontracting has been the availability of low-cost products or processing. In many cases, however, it has led to a remote relationship between customers and suppliers – and not just in terms of physical distance.

Such a system involves firms in holding large stocks or inventories of materials and components in order to insure against interruptions in supply or faulty components. Schonberger (1982) has called this a 'just-in-case' system.

Recently, however, there has been a move towards a very different kind of procurement system with very different relationships between customers and suppliers. The *just-in-time system* (JIT)

> ... emerged in the post-war period as Japanese car manufacturers – particularly Toyota – attempted to adapt US practices to Japanese conditions. Just-in-time is first and foremost a novel form of integrating the parts of a manufacturing system, involving an approach to time economy different than that of JIC. It is literally a system in which tasks are done just when needed, in just the amount required to meet desired output levels.
>
> *(Sayer and Walker 1991, pp. 170–1).*

A key question, therefore, is whether a move towards a JIT system will lead to a reduction in international subcontracting and the revival of localized agglomerations. The likelihood seems to be a mixture of arrangements involving both long- and short-distance linkages depending upon the particular circumstances in specific industries and firms.

One undoubted development is the tendency for many firms to move towards closer functional relationships with their suppliers. Rather than merely seeking out the lowest-cost supplier and little else, there is a strong move towards the nomination of 'preferred suppliers' with whom very close relationships are developed. Such suppliers are increasingly being given greater responsibility for the quality of their outputs and, indeed, are playing a more direct role in the design of products. More generally, a procuring firm has a variety of options in relation to its suppliers. It can opt for single sourcing to gain economies of scale (and lower costs) but with the risk of putting all its procurement eggs in a single supply basket. Alternatively, it can opt for dual or multiple sourcing and spread its subcontracting network more widely.

Activity 3 _____

What are the major trends in the geographical relationship between customers and suppliers in your organization? Is there a move towards JIT methods? If not, why do you think that is so?

Comment _____

Whereas once at the OU we defined our customers only as individuals within the UK, we now see customers as living almost anywhere in the world. Suppliers continue to be located (for course production) in and around Milton Keynes, while suppliers for tutorial support are located where the customers are. As a service, JIT is not an issue with which we have had to deal. Thus, tutors may show up 'just in time' for tutorials, but this is not the meaning of the term.

From the standpoint of our production of learning materials, we have been moving to reducing inventory holding costs by changing our publishing technology to include more electronically accessible text, but this is still far from a JIT system. At some point, it may be possible to have the technology to print 'one-offs' of course materials, but this is still far from the reality of our production methods.

The barriers to JIT production in the OU are considerable. Our production systems are based on ponderous and sometimes overly complex networks of relationships with suppliers (both internal and external), and I would guess that major changes in our processes would be needed before we could ever develop these relationships to the point where JIT worked for us.

2.7 SYNTHESIS OF ORGANIZATIONAL AND GEOGRAPHICAL RELATIONSHIPS

The combination of these various networks of relationships, both within firms and between independent and quasi-independent firms, creates a highly complex geographical structure. The overall scale of this structure is, of course, global but the substructures and the links between them operate at all geographical scales down to the local. Indeed, it is at the local scale 'on the ground' that the processes within the production chain are actually performed. In fact, as I suggested in Section 1.3, the very character of places exerts a considerable influence on the processes and networks I have been discussing. Specifically, geographical relationships within and between clusters of economic activity are, in themselves, an intrinsic part of the production system.

It is a mistake, therefore, to argue that the map of economic activity, at whatever geographical scale, is merely the result of decisions made by business firms (or any other organization) projected on to the Earth's surface. As Walker has rightly observed:

... it is impossible to separate the organizational from the geographical, much less to treat industrial location as the simple outcome of organizational forms or decisions ... space is ... basic to human action ... all forms of organization are inherently spatial to some degree.

(Walker, 1988, p. 385)

Thus the global economy is made up of a variety of complex organizational networks – the internal networks of international firms, the networks of strategic alliances, of subcontracting relationships and of other, newer, organizational forms – which intersect with geographical networks structured particularly around linked agglomerations or concentrations of activities.

The most important point to emphasize is the variety and diversity of processes and outcomes, both organizational and geographical. The production chain can be articulated in different organizational and geographical ways involving networks of both intra- and inter-firm relationships. Such relationships add to the kaleidoscopic complexity of the global economy, in particular because some of them tend to be highly localized (or concentrated) geographically within the global system. Both internal and external relationships are the threads through which the global economy is integrated, linking together both organizations and geographical areas in complex, interrelated and overlapping divisions of labour.

International firms are the most important driving force in these networks. They not only directly control and co-ordinate their own complex internal networks on an international or a global scale but also indirectly control many of the external networks in which they are embedded. The precise form and articulation of production chains and networks is strongly influenced, although not necessarily determined, by technology. Technologies specific to a particular production chain influence both the extent to which the chain may be fragmented in a technical sense and also the degree of flexibility within and between stages in the chain. The more general space-shrinking technologies of transport and communication determine the potential geographical scale on which the production chain can be distributed. However, the precise form and articulation of production networks is also determined by the actions of nation states as they pursue, in particular, policies of trade management and attempt to impose performance requirements on international firms operating within their territories.

The shape of the global economy, then, is the outcome of the complex interplay between the strategies of international firms and nation states set within the context of technological change. The particular mix varies substantially from one industry to another. Geographically, the global economy is made up of intricately interconnected localized clusters of activity which are embedded in various ways into different forms of corporate network which, in turn, vary greatly in their geographical extent. Some TNCs are globally extensive, others have a more restricted geographical span. Either way, however, firms in specific places – and, therefore, the places themselves – are increasingly connected into international and global networks.

2.8 CONCLUSION

This section has aimed to help you understand the ways in which the activities of international business firms may be organized and reorganized geographically. The key to such understanding is the production or value-added chain, which focuses attention on the individual components of an industry or an enterprise and on the relationships between them. The precise geographical configuration of a production chain at a particular time is the result of the interrelated operation of three major factors: technology, the strategic orientation of the firm, and the prevailing political environment. Each element in the production chain has specific locational requirements which may result in either a geographically concentrated or a geographically dispersed pattern. All firms are embedded in complex networks of external relationships, for example, the relationships between customers and suppliers. The nature and the geography of these relationships appear to be changing and moving towards closer functional – and, in some cases, closer geographical – ties. The complex internal and external networks of relationships within and between firms are produced by, and produce, distinctive geographies of production and distribution.

3 THE GEOGRAPHICAL DYNAMICS OF POPULATION AND HUMAN RESOURCES

In many ways, it could be argued that population is the most important basic resource of all. More particularly, in today's highly competitive global environment, *human resources* may well be the major source of international competitive advantage. This is an issue that is discussed in detail in the People unit. Increasingly, it is the knowledge and skills of the population that underpin successful business activity for both firms and geographical areas. At the same time, population size and composition (weighted by income) is the basic determinant of market demand. The subject of population is huge and complex. In this section we focus on just two major aspects: the importance of population to product markets and labour markets.

3.1 THE 'NUMBERS GAME': THE DYNAMICS OF POPULATION CHANGE

The explosive growth of world population

Millions of words have been written about world population growth but the basic message, as we saw in the introductory unit, is very simple.

- In historical terms, the population growth explosion has occurred only in the last 250 years and has been associated with a combination of economic, social and cultural processes.

- The geographical focus of the most rapid population growth has shifted from 'the North' to 'the South' and there is now a major divide between countries with a predominantly 'young' population structure and those whose population structure is 'ageing'.

Figure 11(a) (overleaf) illustrates the first of these two points. It shows that, for almost the whole of human history, population growth rates were very low. In fact, more than 80 per cent of total world population growth has taken place in less than 0.1 per cent of human history. This *population explosion* obviously poses immense problems now and in the future. One estimate is that the next 1 billion people will be added to the Earth's population in a mere 11 years. However, as Figure 11(b) shows, estimates of future world population growth are, indeed, estimates. Figure 11(b) also shows that virtually all the world's population growth – more than 90 per cent – since around 1950 has been occurring in the developing regions ('the South').

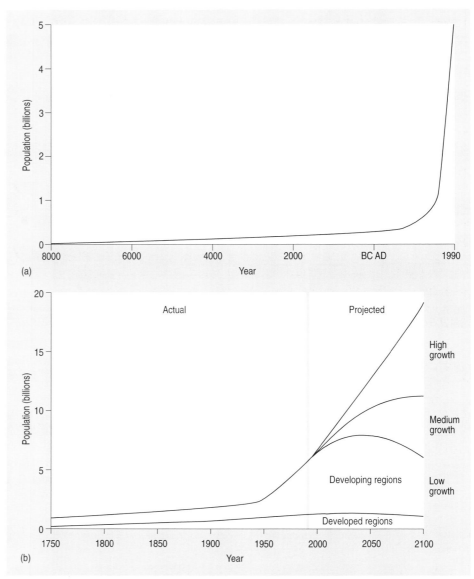

Figure 11   Past and projected population growth rates ((a) Jones, 1990, p. 10; (b) Green, 1992)

Processes of population growth

In any given geographical area, population growth is the result of the interplay between the following components:

- *natural increase* – the relationship between birth (fertility) rates and death (mortality) rates
- *migration* – the net balance between out-migration and in-migration.

If migration is excluded, it has been suggested, countries will tend to proceed through a process of population change over time which has been termed the *demographic transition.* The passage of a country through the stages of the demographic transition is often associated with its process of economic development and its accompanying changes in standards of living, health care and personal aspirations. There is, clearly, some validity in this argument. However, although the demographic transition model is a very useful broad-brush description of the patterns of population change that have occurred in developed countries, it needs to carry a health warning. It does not necessarily follow that *all* countries *will* actually experience exactly the same pattern of transition associated with economic development.

Figure 12 is a simplified view of the demographic transition process. In reality, of course, the birth rate and death rate curves would be far less smooth. The transition process for a particular country can be divided into three broad phases.

Phase I High stationary. In this phase, a country's population remains fairly stable with low net growth rates produced by a combination of high birth rates and high death rates, the latter tending to cancel out or dampen down the former.

Phase II Expansion. In this phase, often linked by demographers to the onset of economic development, the country's population grows in absolute terms. Initially, the growth is stimulated by a fall in the death rate associated with improvements in food supply and quality and in sanitary and health conditions. While birth rates remain high but death rates fall it is obvious that population will grow very rapidly. Eventually, however, it is argued, the birth rate will also begin to decline in association with such societal changes as urban industrial development, higher per capita incomes, higher levels of education, and changing social attitudes towards smaller families.

Phase III Low stationary. In this phase, birth rates and death rates are again more or less in line but at a much lower level than in phase I. In phase III it tends to be the birth rate that fluctuates around a mean level, the fluctuations often being associated with such factors as variations in the business cycle and its effects on perceived job security and prosperity. In contrast, in phase I it is the death rate that tends to fluctuate around a mean, the variations being influenced by such phenomena as famine or plague.

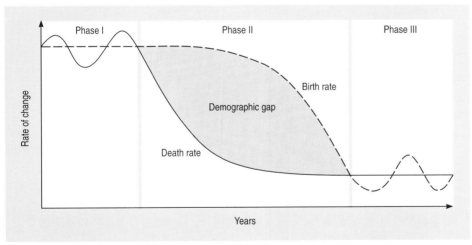

Figure 12   The demographic transition model (Berry *et al.*, 1987, p. 45)

The demographic transition model undoubtedly describes the kinds of population change experienced by the developed, industrialized countries. But the extent to which it applies to today's developing countries is more controversial. Jones (1990) presents a fairly balanced evaluation of this issue:

> ... there are clear relationships in the Third World between levels of development or modernization and levels of mortality and fertility ... The more developed countries have, on the whole, experienced the greatest mortality declines and the beginnings of fertility reduction ...

> But although the early stages of demographic transition may be observed in the Third World, there is no assurance that later stages will replicate European experience and achieve, through fertility regulation,

environmentally sustainable population levels. The other regulation method widely used in Europe – mass emigration to the New World – is unrealistic in today's socio-political climate.

Proponents of demographic regulation as a universally applicable theory suggest optimistically that the necessary rapid fertility regulation can be achieved in the Third World. They point out that latecomers to the transition process, notably Germany, southern and eastern Europe and Japan, all experienced a concentrated and accelerated fertility decline; that, contrary to some views, the pace of modernization in many Third World countries is actually more rapid than in nineteenth-century Europe; and that governments are now prepared and have the capability to promote policies of fertility regulation. There are others who maintain that high fertility is so institutionally interwoven with the entire cultural fabric of less developed countries that its reduction is an intractable problem. The demographic history of the next generation will therefore be of crucial importance.

(Jones, 1990, p. 21)

'Young' populations and 'old' populations

As a result of its specific demographic history, each country develops a particular population age structure. In general, there is a major distinction between the age structure of the developed countries and those of developing countries especially in the proportions of their populations in different age groups.

By way of example, Figure 13 gives a more detailed comparison of the population pyramids for Sweden and for Costa Rica.

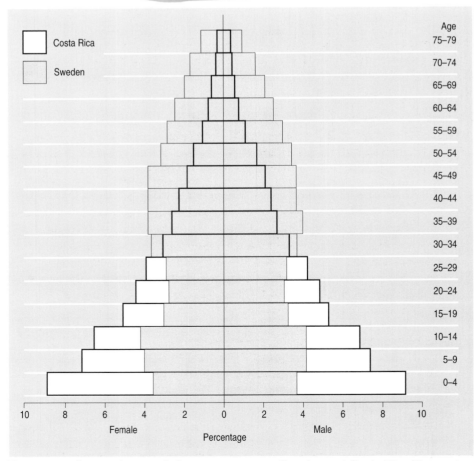

Figure 13   Contrasting population age structures: Sweden and Costa Rica (Berry *et al.*, 1987, p. 45)

By the year 2025, the contrasts will have become much greater. In particular, the percentage of the population aged over 65 years in the developed countries will have grown dramatically although there are considerable variations between individual countries. For example, in Japan the relative size of the over-65 group will have more than doubled, whereas in the UK and Sweden the increase will be more modest because of the already high proportion of their populations over 65. These contrasts in population age structure have immense economic, social and political implications for the countries concerned. For countries with a very young population structure, the immediate problems are the cost and provision of child welfare and education, while the longer-term problems are the effects of this population bulge as it moves through the life-cycle and becomes the source of continuing high levels of fertility and therefore of high rates of population – and labour force – growth. For the developed countries, the problems are rather different. The immediate problems have been providing employment for a large potential labour force which is the result of earlier 'baby booms'. But the imminent problem is one of providing care, including pension provisions, for the rapidly ageing population. Some of the implications for international business of these contrasting age structures are discussed below.

'Mobile' populations: the dynamics of international migration

So far in discussing population change I have assumed that the only influence on a country's population size and structure is natural increase (the net balance of fertility and mortality rates). But there is a further process – *migration* – which may have a major effect on the nature of population change.

Migration can be defined as: a change in a person's place of residence beyond the immediate vicinity of their existing location which results in a break from existing ties of family, work or community. This migration may be permanent or semi-permanent.

Most migration occurs within a person's country of origin, that is, most migration is domestic. But a very significant element is *international migration* across national boundaries. Migration of this type is generally regulated by national governments.

Migration of people is as old as history itself but, as a recent study of mass migration in Europe shows:

> ... international migration is once again of great significance. Both within Europe and beyond, millions are on the move, their journeys reshaping the human mosaic ... Albanian boat people on the Adriatic, Pakistanis occupying a disused spaghetti factory in Rome, Filipinos fleeing an erupting volcano, migrants from the East gathering in the grim splendour of Budapest's railway station – these are just some of the images recalled from the past couple of years. Migration has re-emerged as one of the great challenges of the 1990s ... As the oppressed of the East are lured by the promise of the West, as the impoverished in the South seek a share of the riches of the North, so the political rhetoric takes on a military tone: 'fortress Europe' under siege from the invasion of an army of migrants.
>
> *(King and Öberg, 1993, p. 1)*

Some of the biggest migration flows in recent years have been to the USA, which has operated a more liberal immigration policy than most

European countries, and to Canada and Australia. These last two countries, in particular, have operated a highly selective immigration policy aimed at attracting primarily highly skilled and highly educated migrants. The geographical composition of the migrant population in the USA has changed dramatically during the past few decades. In 1940, for example, about 70 per cent of immigrants originated from the countries of Northern Europe; in 1992 more than 80 per cent originated from Asia, Latin America and the Caribbean.

The actual processes underlying migration are extremely complex, involving economic, social, cultural and political factors in both places of origin and places of destination. Historically (and once again today) a major cause of mass migration has been political or religious persecution – 'ethnic cleansing' to use the currently fashionable, but highly unpleasant, term. Less obvious, but probably more significant overall are the individually smaller, but cumulatively very large, flows of individuals and groups of people seeking a future (whether permanent or temporary) in other countries.

Whatever their specific causes, migration flows can create both benefits and costs for both sending and receiving countries.

3.2 THE IMPLICATIONS OF POPULATION DYNAMICS FOR PRODUCT AND LABOUR MARKETS

The outcomes of the dynamics of population change, especially the processes of migration and changing age composition, have far-reaching implications for society in general. However, from the particular perspective of international business, the dynamics of population change are particularly important in two major respects. First, they affect the size, composition and growth of *product markets.* In a direct sense, the major effect is on consumer goods markets but indirectly, of course, these have an influence on producer goods markets. Second, population dynamics have major implications for *labour markets* and, therefore, for the nature of production itself.

Population influences on consumer markets

The larger a country's population, the larger, potentially, is its consumer market. Marketing managers cast envious eyes on countries like China or India because the sheer size of their populations holds out the promise of huge sales. However, it is obviously not merely a question of numbers of people; what matters is their levels of income and the nature of their consumer preferences. A better rough indicator of market size, therefore, is income per capita as shown in Figure 14.

Per capita income in the high income group of countries in the mid-1990s averaged $23,420; that of the lowest income group was a paltry $380. In fact, the range was much greater than this: from almost $38,000 in Switzerland to $80 in Rwanda (World Bank, 1996). Of course, a consumer market of 1.2 billion people, even with a per capita income of only $530 (the position of China in the mid-1990s) is still a very large market. But there is a further complication: countries with different *income levels* will have different *structures of demand.* The type and mix of goods

Figure 14   World variations in per capita income (Dicken, 1998, p. 189)

demanded tends to vary systematically with income. As incomes rise, so does the aggregate demand for goods and services. But such increased demand does not affect all products in the same way; different goods have different elasticities of demand.

This relationship was first established in the 1850s. Thus, countries with low per capita income levels will spend a high proportion of their income on primary products (basic necessities). Conversely, countries with high income levels will spend a high proportion of their income on 'higher-order' manufactured goods and services. But there is a further factor involved: the *age composition* of the population. As we have seen, there are major differences between countries in this respect. For any given level of income, the tastes and preferences of the young will be very different from those of the middle-aged or the old. They will constitute very different markets. Thus the age structure of a population, along with other social and cultural variables, constitutes one of the major bases of *market segmentation.*

Activity 4 _____

Think of some examples of how consumer product markets may be segmented by age group. How might firms adjust to the changing age composition of their major markets?

Comment

An obvious example is the baby-food market. In the 1970s, the American baby-food maker Gerbers used the slogan, 'Babies are our business, our only business'. As the offspring of the demographic bulge of those born immediately after World War II passed from babies to toddlers, the company kept the slogan, but defined babies to include those under 10 and introduced products aimed specifically at this population.

Population influences on labour markets

People are producers as well as consumers. The size, composition and skill level of a country's population are thus major determinants of the quantity and quality of the available labour force. The large, young, unskilled populations of at least some developing countries, for example, have exerted a major attraction for many firms in recent years. The various 'baby booms' of the developed countries have created a different kind of labour pool and one which is now beginning to decline because of their changing age structures.

Technological changes in production processes and in transport and communications have evened out the significance of geographical location for some of the traditionally important factors of production. Yet labour remains strongly differentiated geographically.

To a very large extent, labour is relatively immobile geographically, although there are important differences in the mobility of different groups. For example, skilled labour is generally more mobile than unskilled labour, male labour is generally more mobile than female labour. Hence the place-specific characteristics of the population are exceptionally important. Of course, labour is not completely immobile; on the contrary, a very large component of international migration is international labour migration. Figure 15 shows the broad patterns of international labour migration flows since the 1960s. But the flow lines of Figure 15 are very broad-brush representations of an extremely complex and internally differentiated reality. Some of the more important underlying factors in labour mobility include:

- *geographical proximity:* most movements are across the nearest border
- *cultural affinities* between areas (language, ethnicity, religion)
- *political relationships* (as in the case of former colonial links or within regional economic blocs such as the EU)
- the *internal labour markets* of international business firms.

Review Question 4

For some activities, international firms frequently operate an internal labour market across national boundaries. How do such labour markets work in practice?

Recently, there has been much speculation about the *globalization* of labour markets but it is important to distinguish between two distinct processes: the geographical mobility of labour itself, and the ability of business firms to seek out appropriate pools of labour on a global scale. There is no doubt about the latter. One of the most significant

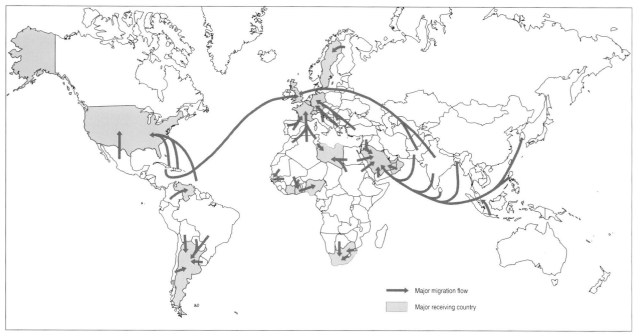

Figure 15   Major international labour migration flows (Dicken, 1992, p. 428; Kols and Lewison, 1983, p. 249)

developments of the period since the early 1960s has been for firms in industries such as textiles, clothing and electronics to locate parts of their value-added chains where they can use either low-cost or specifically skilled labour. But a truly global labour market also implies global mobility of labour itself and here the evidence is less convincing.

On the one hand, Johnston (1991) claims that:

> ... human capital, once considered to be the most stationary factor in production, increasingly flows across national borders as easily as cars, computer chips and corporate bonds ...

> During the 1990s, the world's work force will become even more mobile ...

> The globalization of labor is inevitable.

> *(Johnston, 1991, pp. 115, 126)*

On the other hand, the Commission of the European Communities (1993) finds that, even within the EU – arguably the most integrated international labour market in terms of its regulatory structure – 'there is ... very little movement of labour between Member States' (p. 81).

Of course, there are today, as we have seen, huge flows of international labour migration. But, in reality, these flows affect only a small proportion of the world's labour force. Labour is still relatively immobile 'idiosyncratic and place-bound':

> Local labour markets deserve special emphasis because of labour's relative day-to-day immobility which gives an irreducible role to place-bound homes and communities. For the vast majority of workers, the place of employment lies within the range of the daily journey to work and back.

> *(Storper and Walker, 1989, p. 157)*

Labour is strongly segmented: by location, by skill, by gender.

Activity 5 _____

When you think about your own circumstances, do you regard yourself as 'internationally mobile'? If so, why do you think that? If not, what are the major barriers to your international mobility?

Comment _____

Your answer to this question will probably be quite different from mine. In many ways, I am less internationally mobile than I once was. I have a house, a mortgage, a family who must be considered, and have developed a set of friends whom I would hate to leave behind. On the other hand, I am more suitable for work overseas than I once was. I speak German and French better than I once did, am more capable of adapting to different situations than I once was, and know much more about the world than I once did. Note that the barriers to my mobility would be barriers to relocation even a few miles away, and that the attributes which suit me for greater mobility are unique to an international job. On the whole, I must conclude that I'm internationally mobile, under the right circumstances.

Thus, the geography of labour markets is a kind of nested hierarchy ranging from the local through the national to the global. For some occupations, the relevant labour market is increasingly global in extent but, for the majority, labour markets remain at a much smaller geographical scale. As a result, the specific characteristics of populations in specific places constitute an extremely important influence on business activities.

The important link between people as consumers and people as workers

Throughout this section I have made a distinction between people as consumers, operating in consumer markets, and people as workers, operating in labour markets. But there is, of course, a fundamental link between them. The nature of a particular consumer market depends, as we have seen, on the characteristics of the population, particularly income levels. For most people in modern societies, the primary source of income is employment, that is, participation in the labour market. Consequently, changes in the labour market – for example, those which create or destroy jobs, change their skill content, or raise or lower wages and salaries – will have an impact on the ability and propensity of people to consume.

Despite the consumer boom of the late 1980s, the longer-term trends in the labour markets of the industrialized countries of North America and Europe are disturbing. In terms of unemployment, this is especially so in

Europe where average unemployment rates rose above 12 per cent in the early 1980s, compared with less than 4 per cent in Japan and a little over 5 per cent in the United States. In both the UK and the United States, there has also been a widening of the earnings gap between the highest and lowest paid segments of the labour force. For the first 25 years or so after World War II, the general trend was for the earnings gap between the top and the bottom segments of the labour market to narrow while, at the same time, the overall level of *per capita* income increased substantially. In other words, most people became better off. During recent years, however, this trend towards reducing inequality has been reversed, especially in the United States and the United Kingdom but also in some other countries as well. In 1995, the ratio of the earnings of the highest 10 per cent of the labour force to that of the lowest 10 per cent rose in the United States from 3.2 to 4.4 and in the United Kingdom from 2.4 to 3.4. The average income of the top 5 per cent of US households was roughly seven times that of the bottom 40 per cent of households in the early 1970s. In the mid-1990s, the top 5 per cent earned on average ten times more than the bottom 40 per cent.

The pattern is more mixed across other industrialized countries. It is apparent, for example, that the same degree of increasing income dispersion within the labour force did not occur in many of the continental European countries. In some cases, indeed, the gap narrowed rather than widened. On the other hand, these countries have experienced much higher levels of unemployment than the United States in particular and even the United Kingdom. This suggests that labour market adjustments are occurring in different ways in different countries. In the United States and the United Kingdom, adjustment has been primarily in the form of a relative lowering of wages at the bottom of the scale (i.e. of mainly unskilled workers); in other cases, such wage levels may have been maintained at the expense of jobs. Thus, in both North America and Europe, the gap between high-paid and low-paid workers has widened dramatically. In part, this is linked to education levels: while the average earnings of university and college graduates have increased markedly, the earnings of those workers at the bottom of the skill ladder – those with only the most basic education – have declined, not just in relative terms but, in some cases, in absolute terms as well.

Thus, the answers to the intractable questions of where the jobs will come from and what kinds of jobs they will be are critical. The difficulty is that the causes of these labour market changes are extremely complex and it is extremely difficult to unravel them. The most important components seem to include the following:

- intensifying global restructuring by international business enterprises
- increasing internationalization of production
- technological changes in the production process
- growing import penetration from developing countries.

3.3 CONCLUSION

This section has outlined the critical importance of population distribution, characteristics and dynamics for international business. Population, in the form of human resources, is probably the most important basic resource of all and, increasingly, should be regarded as the most crucial source of international competitive advantage for both firms and countries. Although world population continues to grow at a very high rate there are enormous differences between countries. Some countries – mostly the older industrialized countries – now have an ageing population, while others – primarily the developing and the newly industrializing countries – have a very young population structure. Although people are, in general, relatively immobile over large geographical distances there are, nevertheless, huge international migration flows. These two population variables – the structure of the population and the migration of population – are tremendously important for firms because of their influence on both consumer markets and labour markets.

CONCLUSION TO THE UNIT

The main aim of this unit has been to provide an understanding of why and how geographical processes are important for international business. On the basis of your work on this unit you should now be in a position to answer the following key questions.

- Why is a knowledge of geographical processes important for international business?

- What are the major geographical variables?

- What are the major geographical trends in international business as reflected in changing patterns of FDI?

- How significant is the home country environment for the nature and behaviour of international business firms?

- How do technology, corporate strategy and the political environment affect the geographical configuration of production and value-added chains?

- What are the effects of geography on the relationships between customers and suppliers?

- Why is the geographical concentration of business activities important?

- What are the major components of the dynamics of population change?

- What are the major implications of population dynamics for international business?

If you can answer these questions you will have demonstrated that, as far as international business is concerned, 'geography really does matter'.

REFERENCES

AOKI, A. and TACHIKI, D. (1992) 'Overseas Japanese business operations: the emerging role of regional headquarters', *RIM Pacific Business and Industries,* Vol. 1, pp. 28–39.

BEHRMAN, J.H. and FISCHER, W.A. (1980) *Overseas R & D Activities of Transnational Companies,* Cambridge, Mass., Oelgeschlager, Gunn and Hain.

BERRY, B.J.L., CONKLING, E.C. and RAY, D.M. (1987) *Economic Geography,* Englewood Cliffs, NJ, Prentice Hall.

BRITTON, S. (1990) 'The role of services in production', *Progress in Human Geography,* Vol. 14, pp. 529–46.

COHEN, R.B. (1981) 'The new international division of labour, multinational corporations and the urban hierarchy', in Dear, M. and Scott, A.J. (eds) *Urbanisation and Urban Planning in Capitalist Society,* London, Methuen.

COMMISSION OF THE EUROPEAN COMMUNITIES (1993) *Employment in Europe 1993,* Brussels, Commission of the European Communities.

DANIELS, J.D. and RADEBAUGH, L.H. (1989) *International Business: environments and operations* (5th edn), Reading, Mass., Addison-Wesley.

DICKEN, P. (1998) *Global Shift: Transforming the world economy* (3rd edn), London, Sage.

DICKEN, P. and KIRKPATRICK, C. (1991) 'Services-led development in ASEAN: transnational regional headquarters in Singapore', *The Pacific Review,* Vol. 4, pp. 174–84.

DOZ, Y. (1986) *Strategic Management in Multinational Companies,* Oxford, Pergamon.

DUNNING, J.H. (1979) 'Explaining changing patterns of international production: in defence of the eclectic theory', *Oxford Bulletin of Economics and Statistics,* Vol. 41, pp. 269–96.

FRIEDMANN, J. (1986) 'The world city hypothesis', *Development and Change,* Vol. 17, pp. 69–83.

GRAHAM, S. and MARVIN, S. (1996) *Telecommunications and the City: Electronic spaces, urban places,* London, Routledge.

GREEN, C.P. (1992) *The Environment and Population Growth: Decade for action,* Population Reports, Series M, No. 10, Baltimore, Johns Hopkins School of Public Health, Population Information Program.

HENDERSON, J. and CASTELLS, M. (eds) (1987) *Global Restructuring and Territorial Development,* London, Sage.

HOWELLS, J.R.L. (1990) 'The internationalization of R & D and the development of global research networks', *Regional Studies,* Vol. 24, pp. 495–512.

HU, Y-S. (1992) 'Global firms are national firms with international operations', *California Management Review,* Vol. 34, pp. 107–26.

JOHNSTON, R. and LAWRENCE, P.R. (1988) 'Beyond vertical integration – the rise of the value-adding partnership', *Harvard Business Review*, July–August, pp. 94–101.

JOHNSTON, W.B. (1991) 'Global work force 2000: the new world labor market', *Harvard Business Review*, March–April, pp. 115–27.

JONES, H.R. (1990) *A Population Geography* (2nd edn), London, Paul Chapman.

KING, R. and ÖBERG, S. (1993) 'Introduction: Europe and the future of mass migration', in King, R. (ed.) *Mass Migration in Europe*, London, Belhaven.

KOBRIN, S. J. (1988) 'Strategic integration in fragmented environments: social and political assessments by subsidiaries of multinational firms', in Hood, N. and Vahlne J.E. (eds) *Strategies in Global Competition*, London, Croom Helm.

KOLS, A. and LEWISON, D. (1983) 'Migration, population growth and development', *Population Reports*, Series M-7, Baltimore, Johns Hopkins University.

LEONTIADES, J. (1971) 'International sourcing in the LDCs', *Columbia Journal of World Business*, Vol. VI, No. 6, pp. 19–28.

LYONS, D. and SALMON, S. (1995) 'World cities, multinational corporations, and urban hierarchy: the case of the United States', in Knox, P.L. and Taylor, P.J. (eds) *World Cities in a World-System*, Cambridge, Cambridge University Press, Chapter 6.

MCLUHAN, M. (1967) *The Medium is the Message*, Harmondsworth, Penguin.

MINTZBERG, H. (1973) *The Nature of Managerial Work*, New York, Harper & Row.

OFFICE OF TECHNOLOGY ASSESSMENT (1994) *Multinationals and the National Interest*, Washington, DC, Office of Technology Assessment.

OHMAE, K. (1990) *The Borderless World: Power and strategy in the interlinked economy*, London, Collins.

PATEL, P. (1995) 'Localized production of technology for global markets', *Cambridge Journal of Economics*, Vol. 19, pp. 141–53.

PAULY, L.W. and REICH, S. (1997) 'National structures and multinational corporate behavior: enduring differences in the age of globalization', *International Organization*, Vol. 51, pp. 1–30.

PORTER, M.E. (1986) 'Competition in global industries: a conceptual framework', in Porter, M.E. (ed.) *Competition in Global Industries*, Boston, Harvard Business School Press.

PORTER, M.E. (1990) *The Competitive Advantage of Nations*, London, Macmillan.

RABACK, E. and KIM, E.M. (1994) 'Where is the chain in commodity chains? The service sector nexus', in Gereffi, G. and Korzeniewicz, M. (eds) *Commodity Chains and Global Capitalism*, Westport, Praeger, Chapter 6.

REICH, R. (1991) *The Work of Nations: Preparing ourselves for 21st Century capitalism*, New York, Vintage Books.

ROBOCK, S.H. and SIMMONDS, K. (1989) *International Business and Multinational Enterprises* (4th edn), Homeward, Illinois, Irwin.

SAYER, A. and Walker, R. (1991) *The New Social Economy: Reworking the division of labour,* Cambridge, Mass., Blackwells.

SCHONBERGER, R.J. (1982) *Japanese Manufacturing Techniques: Nine hidden lessons in simplicity,* New York, Free Press.

de SOLA POOL, I. (1981) 'International experts of telecommunications policy', in Moss, M.L. (ed.) *Telecommunications and Productivity,* Reading, Mass., Addison-Wesley, Chapter 7.

STEWART, R. (1983) *Choices for the Manager,* Maidenhead, McGraw-Hill.

STORPER, M. and WALKER, R. (1989) *The Capitalist Imperative: Territory, technology and economic growth,* Oxford, Blackwell.

UNITED NATIONS CENTER ON TRANSNATIONAL CORPORATIONS (UNCTC) (1988) 'Services in the world economy', in *Trade and Development Report 1988, Part Two,* New York, United Nations.

WALKER, R. (1988) 'The geographical organization of production systems', *Environment and Planning D: Society and space,* Vol. 6, pp. 377–408.

WARF, B. (1989) Telecommunications and the globalization of financial services', *Professional Geographer,* Vol. 41, pp. 257–71.

WHITLEY, R. (ed.) (1992a) *European Business Systems: Firms and markets in their national contexts,* London, Sage.

WHITLEY, R. (1992b) *Business Systems in East Asia: Firms, markets and societies,* London, Sage.

WORLD BANK (1996) *World Development Report 1996,* New York, Oxford University Press.

COMMENTS ON REVIEW QUESTIONS

Review Question 1

The intuitive answer to this question is that shrinking geographical distances make geography more important. Consider the arguments for convergence in the Culture unit. One could suggest that, as the world becomes 'smaller', so too, in the long run, it becomes more similar. As it becomes more similar, place could matter more (in that the unique features of place could become more important if they created strong competitive advantage) or less (if the space-shrinking technologies also reduced differences). But also remember I said above that 'a geographical perspective ... emphasizes the interaction between economic, social, political and cultural factors in specific places' (p. 6). Thus, no matter whether convergence is actually occurring or not, a geographical perspective is important.

Review Question 2

The Government unit identifies the following types of activity which have a bearing on this question:

- *trade and tariff issues like tariffs, domestic ownership and domestic content*

- *rules, regulations and procedures*

- *taxation*

- *mergers and acquisitions and competition policy*

- *legal practices*

- *codes of conduct.*

If you want to refresh your memory, you may wish to review the Government unit.

Review Question 3

To answer this, you need to tap your understanding of organizational behaviour. For example, studies of managerial behaviour in the UK and the USA by Rosemary Stewart (1983) and Henry Mintzberg (1973) have suggested that managers prefer short personal contacts with each other. As Marshall McLuhen pointed out in The Medium is the Message (1967), messages sent using the written word are different from ones delivered face to face. Technology will probably have an influence on the degree of face-to-face contact necessary but, as you will probably know by now from your computer work with the course, it is unlikely to replace them entirely. There are social as well as informational needs which are met by communication in person.

Review Question 4

It has been suggested that certain professions operate within different geographical market-places. You need only compare your local newspaper with a national or international one to see that some types of jobs are advertised locally, while others are advertised internationally. The more specialized the job, the more scarce are the possible job holders and the more widely dispersed is the geographical extent of the labour market. It is not only in new posts where international labour markets exist. Some global firms post openings (sometimes on electronic bulletin boards) for jobs throughout the firm, no matter where they are located.

To gain a richer understanding of this question, you will have to wait for the People unit later in the course.

ACKNOWLEDGEMENTS

Grateful acknowledgement is made to the following sources for permission to reproduce material in this unit:

Illustrations

Front cover: NASA; *Figures 2, 3, 4, 6, 7, 8, 9, 14 and 15*: Reprinted by permission of Sage Publications Ltd from Dicken, P., *Global Shift*, 3rd edition, 1998; *Figure 5*: McHale, J. (1969) *The Future of the Future*, George Braziller; *Figure 10: Trade and Development Report 1988*, Part 2, United Nations Center on Transnational Corporations, © United Nations 1988; *Figure 11*: (a) Jones, H.R. (1990) *A Population Geography*, 2nd edition, © 1990 Paul Chapman Ltd, London; (b) *Population Reports*, series M, No. 10 (1992) Johns Hopkins University; *Figures 12 and 13*: Berry, B.J.L., Conkling, E.C. and Ray, D.M. (1987) *Economic Geography*, Prentice Hall Inc.

Tables

Table 1: Robock, S.H. and Simmonds, K. (1989) *International Business and Multinational Enterprises*, Richard D. Irwin Inc.; *Table 2*: Reprinted by permission of Sage Publications Ltd from Dicken, P., *Global Shift*, 3rd edition, 1998; *Table 3*: Whitley, R. (ed.) (1992) *European Business Systems: Firms and markets in their national contexts*, Sage Publications Ltd.